MICHIGAN'S ECONOMIC FUTURE

CHALLENGES AND OPPORTUNITIES

CHARLES L. BALLARD

Michigan State University Press • *East Lansing*

Michigan State University Press
East Lansing, Michigan 48823-5245
www.msupress.msu.edu

Printed and bound in the United States of America.

12 11 10 09 08 07 06   1 2 3 4 5 6 7 8 9 10

LIBRARY OF CONGRESS CATALOGING-IN-PUBLICATION DATA
Ballard, Charles L.
Michigan's economic future : challenges and opportunities / Charles L. Ballard.
p. cm.
ISBN-13: 978-087013-796-9 (pbk. : alk. paper)
ISBN-10: 0-87013-796-4 (pbk. : alk. paper)
1. Michigan—Economic conditions. 2. Michigan—Economic policy. I. Title.
HC 107.M5B35 2006
330.9774—dc22
2006021411

Cover and book design by Sharp Des!gns, Inc., Lansing, Michigan

g green press INITIATIVE Michigan State University Press is a member of the Green Press Initiative
and is committed to developing and encouraging ecologically responsible
publishing practices. For more information about the Green Press Initiative and the use of
recycled paper in book publishing, please visit *www.greenpressinitiative.org.*

Visit Michigan State University Press on the World Wide Web at *www.msupress.msu.edu*

For Shirley

Contents

Acknowledgments

From 2000 until 2003, I was involved in writing and editing *Michigan at the Millennium*, a volume of research papers on the Michigan economy. Lou Anna K. Simon, the president of Michigan State University, expressed a desire for a shorter book about Michigan's economy, to follow up on the success of *Michigan at the Millennium*. Dr. Simon provided early guidance and encouragement, and she provided the resources that have made this book possible. Thus, my first debt is to Dr. Simon.

I would also like to thank Fred Bohm and Julie Loehr of the Michigan State University Press, who worked with me throughout the development of this book.

I am grateful to Rowena Pecchenino, Margaret Lynch, and Belen Feight, all of the Department of Economics at Michigan State University, for facilitating this project.

In addition, I would like to thank the other editors of *Michigan at the Millennium*, whose efforts contributed so greatly to the high quality of the volume: Paul Courant and Liz Gerber of the University of Michigan, Doug Drake of Public Policy Associates (formerly of Wayne State University), and Ron Fisher of Michigan State University.

I am also grateful to the people who provided helpful comments on drafts of the chapters in this book. Liz Gerber deserves a special thanks for her many helpful comments on the drafts of several chapters. Thanks also to Tom Clay, Adam Cogswell, Stacy Dickert-Conlin, Doug Drake, Michael Gallagher, Stu Paterson, and Earl Ryan.

My thanks also go to Tim Bartik, Nate Bedocs, Dale Belman, Becky Blank, Rich Block, Ken Boyer, Sheldon Danziger, Scott Darragh, Peter Eisinger, Jeff Guilfoyle, Steve Haider, Gloria Helfand, Jim Hines, Larry Martin, Jack Meyer, Leslie Papke, Doug Roberts, Joel Slemrod, Steve Woodbury, and John Wolfe, all of whom provided helpful comments and suggestions. A special thank-you goes to John Goddeeris, who wrote the chapter on health issues in *Michigan at the Millennium*, and was also instrumental in getting me involved in the project in the first place.

Toward the end of the process of writing this book, I had the pleasure of participating in "Where Do We Go From Here? An Agenda-Setting Conference for the Issues Facing Michigan," held in Ann Arbor on March 14, 2006. I had stimulating conversations about Michigan's economy with dozens of other conference participants, some of whom I have already thanked. Other conference participants whose remarks were valuable to me include Essel Bailey, Mary Sue Coleman, James Duderstadt, Paul Dimond, Randy Eberts, George Erickcek, George Fulton, Lou Glazer, David Hollister, Doug Rothwell, Craig Ruff, and James Sallee. Special thanks to Liz Gerber and Phil Power, the conference organizers, who were kind enough to invite me.

Education will play an extremely important role in shaping Michigan's future, and this book deals with education policy issues in some detail. My views on higher education have been shaped by many of the folks whom I have already thanked. Also, in the past few years I have had many very useful conversations with parents, administrators, and members of the school board in East Lansing. I am especially grateful to Rima Addiego, Kay Biddle, Jeff Biddle, David Chapin, Babs Krause, Daphne O'Regan, Paula Steele, Rodney Stokes, Paula Weiner, and George Wyatt.

In recent years, I have had the opportunity to discuss the Michigan economy with reporters from the broadcast and print media. These conversations have helped to shape my understanding of the issues. I have done too many of these interviews to thank everyone here, but I would specifically like to thank Louis Aguilar, Chris Andrews, Rick Haglund, Kathy Hoffman, Chris Holman, Brandon Lenoir, Jack Lessenberry, Stefanie Murray, Charity Nebbe,

Rick Pluta, Jeremy Ross, Garrison Wells, and Barbara Wieland. Thanks to MSU's Russ White for facilitating contacts with the news media.

Last, but not least, thanks to Shirley and the boys for putting up with me.

All of these people deserve some of the credit for this book. Any errors are my responsibility alone.

Introduction

I n 2003, the Michigan State University Press published *Michigan at the Millennium: A Benchmark and Analysis of Its Fiscal and Economic Structure*. This landmark work was sponsored by Michigan State University, the University of Michigan, and Wayne State University, with additional financial support from the Charles Stewart Mott Foundation. It includes 33 chapters, covering nearly every aspect of economic life in Michigan. Because of its exhaustive coverage, *Michigan at the Millennium* is an essential reference work.

However, there is a downside to this level of detail: *Michigan at the Millennium* is more than 700 pages long. In writing this new book, my goal is to provide readers with a short introduction to many of the issues covered in its larger companion. It is also hoped that this book will stimulate some readers to turn to *Michigan at the Millennium* for more in-depth analysis.

Of course, the world has not stood still in the three years since *Michigan at the Millennium* was published. In this book, I also use more recent information to discuss some of the latest policy controversies.

Some Key Themes of This Book

Rather than summarize all of the details here, I will use the rest of this introduction to set the stage by briefly discussing a few issues and ideas of central importance.

The Decline of Manufacturing

A century ago, Michigan's economy was dominated by agriculture, but massive changes were under way. There was an opportunity to create a more prosperous future in an economy based on manufacturing. Visionaries like Henry Ford, R. E. Olds, and Herbert Dow turned that opportunity into reality for Michigan. By the middle of the twentieth century, Michigan was an industrial powerhouse, and our economy was the envy of the world.

However, manufacturing's share of the economy has been shrinking for several decades, both in Michigan and in the rest of the United States. This long transition has been more painful for Michigan than for most of the United States, because manufacturing was (and still is) a much larger portion of the economy in Michigan than in the average state. In a sense, we have been the victims of our own success. Michigan rode the wave of manufacturing more successfully than almost anyone else. As a result, however, the transition out of manufacturing has been more difficult for the people of Michigan.

Of course, manufacturing will continue to be a very important part of Michigan's economy for many years to come. But all of the evidence points to a more prosperous future in skill-intensive, knowledge-driven sectors of the economy.

The manufacturing economy is discussed in considerable detail in two of the chapters in *Michigan at the Millennium*. One of these is an overview of the Michigan economy by Joan Crary, George Fulton, and Saul Hymans of the University of Michigan. The other, which focuses on manufacturing in general, and the automobile industry in particular, is by Richard Block and Dale Belman of Michigan State University. I will discuss the decline of manufacturing in more detail in the next chapter.

The Widening Gap between Rich and Poor

The American economy enjoyed tremendous success from the end of the Second World War to the middle 1970s. The economy experienced rapid economic growth, and the gains were shared throughout the population. Incomes grew for those at the bottom and middle of the economic ladder, as well as for those at the top.

Since about 1975, however, the distribution of income has become more and more unequal. The top 20 percent of households have seen huge increases in their incomes. On the other hand, incomes have grown much more slowly, if at all, for those in the middle and at the bottom. The wages of college-educated workers have surged ahead, while the wages of those with only a high-school diploma have stagnated, and the wages of high-school dropouts have plummeted.

There are many reasons for the widening gap between those at the top and those at the bottom. However, the number-one cause is an increase in employers' demand for highly skilled workers. Changes in technology have tended to favor workers who have high levels of education and training.[1]

The Crucial Role of Highly Skilled Workers

It was once perfectly sensible for young Michigan residents to say, "I'll get one of those high-paying factory jobs, so I don't need a college education." For the vast majority of today's young people, however, the old days are gone, and they are not coming back. If today's young people are to compete effectively in the global marketplace, they must have strong skills. However, Michigan lags behind the rest of the country in the percentage of its population with a college education.

Unfortunately, it appears that much of the Michigan public is in denial about the problem. Our public policies toward higher education would seem to indicate that we are becoming *less* interested in providing our people with skills. Michigan's budget for higher education has been slashed repeatedly in recent years. The State of Michigan supports 15 four-year institutions of higher learning. The budget cuts have been spread across all fifteen. However, the total size of the cuts is equivalent to the *complete elimination* of the state's support for *seven* of these universities.

Fortunately, it also appears that a growing number of Michigan citizens do recognize the seriousness of the situation. For example, there is the Lt. Governor's Commission on Higher Education and Economic Growth (the "Cherry Commission"), which produced its report in December 2004.[2] I will discuss the Cherry Commission's ideas in more detail in chapter 2. For now, I quote a key passage from the Cherry Commission Report:

Michigan's residents, businesses, and governments can either move forward to a future of prosperity and growth fueled by the knowledge and skills of the nation's best-educated population, or they can drift backward to a future characterized by ever-diminishing economic opportunity, decaying cities, and population flight—a stagnant backwater in a dynamic world economy.

In this book, I will make the case for an enhanced commitment to investments in education. The details of the argument are mostly in chapter 2. For now, however, I want to emphasize that I am *not* referring only to the four-year universities. We do not merely need to increase the number of Michigan residents with a bachelor's degree. Rather, we need to enhance education, training, and skills throughout the entire spectrum. We need to start at the very beginning, with early-childhood education and solid instruction in elementary school. We need to decrease the number of high-school dropouts. We need to make sure that those who receive a high-school diploma have truly received a high-school education.[3] And we need to increase the number who go on to some sort of additional education or training, which could take the form of job-skills training, or study at a community college, or study at a university.

How Do We Pay for Increased Investments in Education?

The Cherry Commission Report makes a compelling case for increasing the skills of the Michigan population. If we are to make progress along those lines, it will take more resources. We will need more classrooms, more laboratories, more computers, more instructors, and so on. The Cherry Commission does not address the question of how to pay for those additional resources, but it is a question that must be addressed.

If we are to increase our investment in education, how will we pay for it? Some might say that we can substantially increase the number of students without spending any more money. In my opinion, however, that would be a self-defeating strategy, because it would force us to sacrifice the *quality* of education. If we are to maintain quality (which is essential) while increasing the *quantity* of education, then it will be necessary to devote more money to education. This, in turn, will necessitate some changes in the government budget. We can either reduce spending on other activities of government, or we can increase the total amount of resources available for public programs.

It may be possible to make some spending cuts elsewhere in the budget. In particular, spending on the corrections system is much higher in Michigan than in comparable states, so a case can be made for a reduction in spending on prisons. However, even if we make substantial reductions in the rest of the budget, they will not be large enough to make room for the necessary amount of educational investment. (Note that, with the exception of corrections, many of the programs in the state budget have already gone through major reductions in recent years. Also, tremendous spending pressures are looming on the near horizon. For example, as we will see in chapter 2, the health-insurance programs for retired public employees have tens of billions of dollars of unfunded liabilities.) Thus, a major part of the financing of increased investments in education must come from increasing the resources available for public programs. If that is to occur, it will be necessary to increase tax revenues.

Recently, I was discussing some of these issues in an undergraduate classroom. I explained that I could not see any way to do what needs to be done, without additional resources. One of my students asked, "So you're saying we should spend more on education, and we should raise taxes to pay for it?" The answer is yes. The student then said that such a strategy would be political suicide.

I have thought a lot about that conversation, and especially about "political suicide." Undoubtedly, there will be political opposition to devoting additional resources to education. But if it really is political suicide to do what needs to be done for the future of Michigan's economy, then we are dead already.

The Weaknesses of Michigan's Tax System

The Michigan tax system is among the most important subjects in *Michigan at the Millennium*. The book devotes several chapters to taxes, including separate chapters on the income tax, the sales tax, property taxes, the Single Business Tax, and other revenue sources. I will discuss Michigan's state and local tax systems in detail in chapter 5 of this book. For now, it will suffice to make a few points about Michigan's tax system.

- *The tax system in Michigan is slowly being eaten away, like a house full of termites.*
  Because of structural flaws in the taxes we use in Michigan, the system is

losing more and more revenue every day, even when there are no changes in the tax laws. (As we shall see in chapter 5, the termites are at work in *all* of the major taxes in Michigan, including the sales tax, the income tax, the property tax, and the taxes on beer, wine, tobacco products, and motor fuels.) On top of that, the laws have been changed in recent years in ways that cause further hemorrhaging of tax revenues. To carry forward the termite analogy: at the very same time that the termites are eating away at the foundation of the house, we have deliberately subjected parts of the house to the wrecking ball.

As a result of the termites and wrecking balls, the overall level of tax revenues is down substantially in recent years. The percentage of income paid in taxes in Michigan is now at its lowest level in decades. If that percentage were to return to its average level of the last generation, about $5 billion per year in additional revenues would be available for public programs. If we were to return to the level of 30 years ago, the additional revenue would be about $10 billion per year. Thus, when I say we need more revenues, I am *not* calling for taxes in Michigan to rise to unprecedented levels. Instead, I am calling for a return to something closer to a level of taxation under which Michigan residents have prospered in the past.

- *Michigan's tax system is one of the most regressive in the country.* A "regressive" tax system is one that takes a higher percentage from low-income residents than from those with high incomes. There are several reasons for this, including the fact that Michigan's income tax has a single flat rate on all taxable income, in contrast to the graduated-rate systems that are used in most other states.

- *Moreover, Michigan's tax system has become more regressive in recent years.* If we look at the major tax-policy changes of the last 12 years, they all have one thing in common: all have the effect of increasing the taxes on low-income Michigan residents, relative to the taxes of those with high incomes. For example, the income-tax rate has been reduced six times, while the retail sales-tax rate has been increased substantially.

Thus, we are faced with a great irony. As mentioned earlier, the distribution of income has become more and more unequal during the last 30 years. Many of those with the highest incomes have become even more affluent, while many of those with the lowest incomes have suffered a declining standard of living. At the same time, the fortunate folks at the top have been paying a smaller and smaller relative share of the taxes in Michigan. The ability to pay taxes has become increasingly concentrated at the top of the income scale, and yet the actual taxes paid have become more concentrated at the bottom.

For these reasons, I say that the *income tax* should play a prominent role in fixing the structural budget deficits that have plagued the State of Michigan in recent years. Of course, the income tax does not have to be the only solution to the budgetary problems. In chapter 5, I will discuss reforms to a wide variety of additional revenue sources, including the dilapidated sales tax. But the income tax is the only source of revenue that is deliberately designed with the idea of taxing people according to their ability to pay. In view of the increased level of inequality, it is common sense to ask those at the top of the income scale to pay their share.

I hasten to add that I do not make this recommendation lightly. First of all, let's face it: nobody likes to pay taxes, myself included. Also, much of my research career has been devoted to thinking about the negative effects of taxes on the economy.[4] Taxes can cause people to reduce their work effort, or to reduce their savings and investment, or to make other undesirable changes in their behavior. These changes in behavior impose real costs on society. However, it is important to keep these costs in perspective. The goal of fiscal policy is not to eliminate taxes. Rather, the goal is to find the correct balance between the benefits of public programs and the costs of the taxes that are used to finance them. In the Michigan economy of today, the benefits of educational investments are enormous. In my judgment, those benefits are large enough to justify an increased investment in education, even though it will be necessary to pay for it.

A Perspective on Policy Analysis and Policy Advocacy

As one of the editors of *Michigan at the Millennium*, I was involved in a variety of decisions about what to emphasize in the book. We decided to ask our authors to concentrate on public-policy analysis, and not to push too hard on particular policy recommendations. Our goal was to provide a sound basis for understanding the Michigan economy, but to let readers reach their own policy conclusions.

There is a great deal of policy analysis in this book, just as in *Michigan at the Millennium*. However, I also offer a number of policy recommendations. These recommendations are my own. They do not necessarily represent the views of Michigan State University, or the MSU Department of Economics, or the other editors of *Michigan at the Millennium*, or the authors of the chapters in *Michigan at the Millennium*.

What's to Come?

If I could accomplish one goal with this book, it would be to convince my readers of the seriousness of Michigan's economic situation, and the need to adapt to new circumstances. Half a century ago, the world was knocking on Michigan's door. But yesterday is gone, and it is not coming back. If the people of Michigan are to achieve a brighter economic future, we will need to develop new ways of thinking, and new ways of engaging with the rapidly changing global economy. Policy discussions in Michigan often have a tinge of complacent nostalgia for the economy of the 1950s and 1960s. It is time to shed those attitudes and replace them with a new set of attitudes—creative, highly skilled, flexible, and entrepreneurial. If we can make the transition to a new mindset, we really can achieve a vibrant economic future for Michigan.

With those ideas in mind, here is the plan for the rest of this book:

- *Chapter 1.* I consider the overall structure of the Michigan economy. I take a longer look at the growth and shrinkage of various industries, as well as the trends in employment and income. I also stress the importance of Michigan's economic connections with the rest of the United States, and with the rest of the world.
- *Chapter 2.* I focus on human resources. In particular, I look at Michigan's population, work force, and education system. I have already stressed the importance of education and training, and I elaborate on those ideas in chapter 2. I deal with K–12 education and the higher-education system.
- *Chapter 3.* I examine physical resources, especially the related issues of environment, land use, and transportation. Michigan's road system is not in very good shape, and there is evidence that we could provide for surface transportation more efficiently than we do now. One of the biggest issues facing Michigan is how to preserve open space while still housing a growing population.

- *Chapter 4.* I consider some issues of public expenditure and public policy that have not been emphasized in the earlier chapters. These include corrections, health care, income-maintenance programs, and unemployment insurance.
- *Chapter 5.* I deal with the tax system. I have already argued that the income tax has an especially important role to play, but I also discuss reforms of several other taxes. In Michigan, as in other states, the sales tax involves very little taxation of services. This causes an inefficient distortion of economic activity. Also, since services have been growing faster than other parts of the economy, the nontaxation of services has contributed to Michigan's chronic budgetary problems. The Single Business Tax (SBT) is a perennial source of controversy. I discuss the possibilities for reform or elimination of the SBT.
- *Chapter 6.* I provide a conclusion.

These are exciting times for anyone interested in economic policy issues in Michigan. I hope you will read on.

NOTES

1. An excellent discussion of the national trends in the income distribution can be found in Peter Gottschalk's article, "Inequality, Income Growth, and Mobility: The Basic Facts," *Journal of Economic Perspectives* 11 (1997): 21–40. In their chapters in *Michigan at the Millennium*, Rebecca Blank and George Johnson (both of the University of Michigan) compare the trends in Michigan's income distribution with the trends for the nation as a whole.

2. The Commission's final report is available at *http://www.cherrycommission.org/docs/finalReport/CherryReportFULL.pdf*.

3. For a discussion of the K–12 education system in Michigan, see the chapter in *Michigan at the Millennium* by Julie Cullen and Susanna Loeb.

4. For example, see Charles Ballard, John Shoven, and John Whalley, "General Equilibrium Computations of the Marginal Welfare Costs of Taxation in the United States," *American Economic Review* 75 (1985): 128–138, and Ballard and Don Fullerton, "Distortionary Taxes and the Provision of Public Goods," *Journal of Economic Perspectives* 6 (1992): 117–131.

An Overview of the Michigan Economy

T his book is concerned with the economic policy issues facing Michigan. However, before we can dive into policy discussions, we need a basic understanding of the facts of the economy. What's big? What's little? What's growing? What's shrinking? The purpose of this chapter is to provide some of those basic facts, in five areas:

- First, we look at the industrial composition of Michigan's economy and compare it with the economy of the United States as a whole. We also look at the long-term decline of the manufacturing sector. Michigan is involved in manufacturing to a far greater degree than most other states. Thus, the decrease in the relative importance of manufacturing is key to many of Michigan's economic problems.
- Second, we look at the trends in employment and unemployment. For the Michigan labor market, the recovery from the 2001 recession has been very slow. Consequently, the Michigan unemployment rate has been above the national rate for several years. However, the gap between Michigan and the rest of the country is smaller than it was in the 1970s and 1980s, when Michigan's unemployment rates were extremely high.
- Third, we look at incomes. Per capita income in Michigan has grown substantially over the last half-century, but the rate of growth has been less rapid in Michigan than in the rest of the United States. Until the early

1980s, per capita income in Michigan was consistently above the U.S. average. For most of the last 25 years, however, Michigan incomes have been below the national average. We also look at the trend toward greater income inequality.

- Fourth, we look at the economic connections between Michigan and the rest of the United States. Michigan's economy is very closely interconnected with the rest of the country. This makes the people of Michigan much more prosperous than they would be if they were cut off from the other 49 states. However, it also means that Michigan's economic performance depends a great deal on things over which people in Michigan have little control.

- Finally, we look at the connections between Michigan and the rest of the world. Largely because of our closeness to Canada, Michigan has greater international connections than most other states have. This means that Michigan has much to gain from a strong world economy, and much to lose from excessive restrictions on international trade.

Which Industries Are Most Important to the Michigan Economy?

We begin our tour of Michigan's economy by looking at the relative sizes of various industries in 2003.[1] For each industry in table 1.1, the second column gives the industry's percentage of the Michigan economy. The third column gives the comparable percentage for the United States as a whole. The industries are shown in order of their importance in Michigan.

The first row of table 1.1 shows that the service sector is the largest sector of the Michigan economy. The service sector encompasses a wide range of activities, including legal, medical, management, and accounting services; computer-systems design; performing arts and museums; food services; and many more. The service sector accounts for about 25.6 percent of Michigan's economy, and about 25.2 percent of the economy of the entire United States. Thus, Michigan is a fairly typical state in terms of the fraction of its economy in services. Michigan is also close to the national average in wholesale and retail trade, real estate, state and local government, construction, transportation, and utilities.

However, the second row of table 1.1 shows that Michigan is not at all typical when it comes to manufacturing. Nearly 21 percent of Michigan's economy

TABLE 1.1 Value of Production in Selected Industries, as a Percentage of Total Value of Production, for Michigan and the United States, 2003

INDUSTRY	MICHIGAN	UNITED STATES
Services	25.57	25.22
Manufacturing	20.71	12.84
Durable Goods	16.78	7.30
Motor Vehicle and Parts	10.16	1.12
Nondurable Goods	3.93	5.53
Wholesale and Retail Trade	12.84	12.96
Real Estate, Rental, and Leasing	11.52	12.52
State and Local Government	9.06	8.72
Finance and Insurance	5.89	8.08
Construction	4.45	4.59
Information	2.72	4.52
Transportation and Warehousing	2.48	2.92
Utilities	2.20	2.03
Federal Civilian Government	1.14	2.26
Agriculture, Forestry, Fishing, and Hunting	0.50	1.04
Federal Military	0.18	1.10
Mining	0.17	1.19

Source: http://www.bea.gov/bea/regional/gsp/.

is in manufacturing, while less than 13 percent of the U.S. economy is in that sector. Table 1.1 also shows some detail within the manufacturing sector. It is probably no surprise that Michigan's heavy reliance on manufacturing is concentrated in durable-goods manufacturing, and especially in the automobile industry.

Table 1.1 also shows that several sectors are relatively *smaller* for Michigan than for the United States as a whole. One of these is finance and insurance: none of the nation's leading financial centers is located in Michigan. Another sector where Michigan lags behind the national average is the information industry, which includes publishing, software, motion pictures, broadcasting, and telecommunications. These industries tend to be strongest on the East and West Coasts.

Mining is also relatively small in Michigan. Mining is about 1.2 percent of the national economy, but only about one-sixth of one percent of the economy in Michigan. This is partly due to the relatively small size of the oil industry in Michigan.

Table 1.1 shows that agriculture, forestry, fishing, and hunting make up one-half of one percent of the Michigan economy; this compares with a bit more than one percent of the national economy. Note that these figures do not include food processing and distribution, food retailing, or restaurants and bars, which are included in other sectors. If we were to combine all of these activities into a "food-related" industry, it would be substantially larger. (For example, food-product manufacturing in Michigan is about twice as large as agriculture, and restaurants and bars are more than three times as large as agriculture.) Subject to that clarification, however, it should be clear that agriculture itself is relatively smaller in Michigan than in the rest of the country.

Finally, it is worth noting that the activities of the federal government are small in Michigan relative to the rest of the country. For example, the federal military makes up about one percent of the national economy, but less than one-fifth of one percent of the Michigan economy. This is because most of America's major military installations are in southern and western states.

The Relative Decline of Manufacturing

Table 1.1 has provided a "snapshot" of the Michigan economy in 2003. Figure 1.1 is a "motion picture" of the share of the economy in manufacturing from 1977 to 2003. Throughout this entire period, manufacturing has been a much larger part of Michigan's economy than of the overall U.S. economy. All across the country, however, the trend for manufacturing has been downward. Both for Michigan and for the entire United States, manufacturing's share of the economy was barely more than half as great in 2003 as it had been in 1977.[2]

Figure 1.1 begins in 1977, because high-quality data are readily available in a convenient form for the years since then. However, other data sources indicate that the relative decline of manufacturing has been going on since the 1950s. Thus, Michigan is very heavily involved in a sector of the economy that

FIGURE 1.1 Manufacturing as Percent of Gross Product,
for Michigan and the United States, 1977–2003

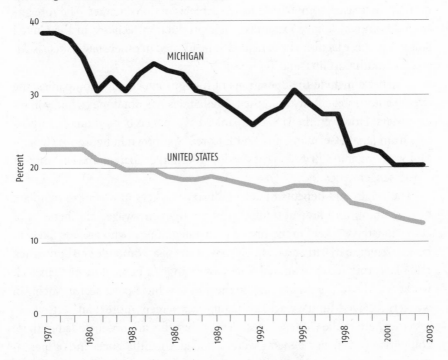

Source: U.S. Department of Commerce, Bureau of Economic Analysis; http://www.bea.gov/bea/regional/gsp.

has been in relative decline for several decades. That simple fact is the source of many of the challenges facing Michigan's economy.

The automobile industry is at the head of the list of manufacturing industries in Michigan. As with so many manufacturing industries, the auto industry has accounted for a shrinking percentage of output and employment in the United States. However, the auto industry has fared worse in Michigan than in the United States as a whole. This is partly because the auto industry in Michigan is dominated by the Big Three U.S. automakers. In the middle of the twentieth century, the Big Three enjoyed a cozy situation. They did not usually compete vigorously with each other, and they faced very little competition from abroad. As a result, they were able to raise car prices to higher levels than could be sustained in a competitive market. The industry was very profitable, and the United Auto Workers were able to capture a portion of the profits. Eventually, however, companies from Japan and other countries brought increased competition to the American auto market. The foreign-owned companies have expanded their production facilities in the United States, but these facilities have tended to be located in other states, such as Alabama, South Carolina, and Tennessee.[3]

When we include the operations of foreign-owned auto companies, the overall automobile industry in the United States has not done so badly in recent years. However, the U.S. companies have lagged behind their competitors from Japan, Germany, and South Korea. As shown in figure 1.2, General Motors, Ford, and Chrysler have steadily lost market share in the U.S. market for passenger cars.[4]

The wages and benefits of auto-industry workers in Michigan (who are heavily unionized) are substantially higher than the wages and benefits of auto-industry workers in the rest of the United States (who are less likely to be union members). In 2004, Michigan workers in automobile and light-truck manufacturing received annual wages averaging 11.7 percent more than such workers in the rest of the country. In the motor-vehicle-parts sector, Michigan workers received annual wages averaging 28.7 percent more than parts workers elsewhere in the United States.[5] (Fringe benefits are not included in these comparisons. If fringe benefits were included, the differences in compensation between auto-industry workers in Michigan and elsewhere would be even greater.)

Increased competition in the auto industry has been great for consumers, who have benefited from lower prices and a wider variety of products. But competition has cut into the profits of the Big Three, which find themselves with a cost structure that cannot be sustained in the face of competition. From 1984 to 2004, auto-industry employment of nonunion workers in America actually increased by about half a million, but auto-industry employment of union members in America fell by about 300,000.

The Transitions in Agriculture and Manufacturing

In many ways, the long-term decline of manufacturing is similar to the earlier decline of agriculture. In the nineteenth century, the Michigan economy was dominated by agriculture. In those days, the average farm worker could only

FIGURE 1.2 Combined Share of the "Big Three" U.S. Automobile Manufacturers in the U.S. Passenger Car Market, 1976–2004

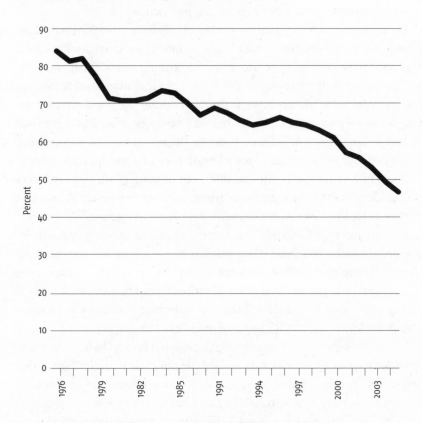

produce enough food to feed a few people. The only way for the population to feed itself was for a large fraction of the labor force to be employed in agriculture.

However, as a result of unprecedented improvements in agricultural productivity (some of which were developed at Michigan Agricultural College and its successors), each farm worker in America today can produce enough to feed several dozen people. This increase in agricultural productivity was essential for the economic development of the United States, because it allowed us to feed ourselves while freeing resources for pursuits other than agriculture. (Around the world today, the most prosperous countries have the smallest percentages of their labor forces in agriculture. On the other hand, most workers in the poorest countries have to be involved in agriculture, because those countries have low agricultural productivity.)

The improvements in agricultural productivity were crucial for economic growth, but they were not painless. As agricultural productivity increased, fewer and fewer workers were needed in the farming sector. (That is the nature of a productivity increase—it allows us to produce more stuff with fewer people.)[6] Millions of Americans left the farm during the twentieth century. Many found new jobs quickly and achieved a new prosperity. But some farm workers encountered a difficult transition in the search for new occupations.

For better or for worse, the long transition out of agriculture has already run most of its course. But the transition out of manufacturing is still very much under way. The two transitions are very similar, in positive ways and in negative ways. Improvements in agricultural productivity paved the way to a higher standard of living, and improvements in manufacturing productivity have had the same beneficial effect. But just as some farm workers were left stranded by the changes in agriculture, so have some factory workers been left stranded by the changes in manufacturing. Since Michigan's economy is so deeply involved in manufacturing, the transition continues to be more difficult for Michigan than for much of the rest of the country.

One of the biggest challenges facing Michigan is how to handle the ongoing transition out of manufacturing. One possibility is to do nothing, other than to hope for the good old days to return. But that would be very unwise. To see why, we only need to recall the history of the transition out of agriculture. One hundred years ago, it would have been unwise to do nothing while merely hoping that the dominance of agriculture would somehow reestablish itself. Instead of hoping for a return of the past, Michigan embraced the future (which, at that time, was in manufacturing). Similarly, today it would be unwise to do nothing while merely hoping that the dominance of manufacturing will reestablish itself. Instead of hoping for a return of the past, Michigan would be smart to embrace the future. Increasingly, future prosperity lies in a more highly skilled work force, and more advanced technologies.

Perhaps the most important challenge facing Michigan today is a psychological one. It will be difficult for our economy to move ahead unless we are mentally prepared to do so. As long as some Michiganians hold onto the false hope that yesterday is coming back, it will hinder our progress toward tomorrow.

Potential Sources of Future Growth

Of course, there is no need to abandon the manufacturing industries that have played such a large role in Michigan's economy in the past. In fact, one of the bright spots of the Michigan economy in recent years has been the growth of automotive high-technology research. In their chapter in *Michigan at the Millennium*, Abel Feinstein, George Fulton, and Donald Grimes show that Michigan has become the world center for automotive engineering, research, and design. (On the other hand, information technology and biotechnology in Michigan have lagged somewhat behind the rest of the country.)

Where else might Michigan find opportunities for growth? First of all, Michigan's economy will be greatly strengthened if we can continue to be a center for industrial high technology, while increasing our share of biotechnology and information technology. The "Life Sciences Corridor" has already begun to reap benefits, and it has tremendous potential for the future.

Alternative energy is another area that is almost certain to grow. Michigan will benefit by increasing its role as a center of alternative-energy research, development, and production. It is hard to say for certain what America's energy system will look like in 20 years. Hydrogen, solar power, wind power, and even fusion may be much bigger players than they are now. But it is safe to say that we will rely less heavily on petroleum than we do now.

One type of alternative energy that bears special mention is bio-based fuel. Corn-based ethanol has great potential for Michigan. Michigan's farmers know how to grow corn, and lots of it. If ethanol were to become a dominant source of energy in the future, it would help to breathe new life into Michigan's agricultural sector. In addition, the technologies for processing and distributing biofuels are certain to continue to change. These ongoing changes will require scientists and engineers. Michigan has an opportunity to grab this bull by the horns, in a way that can provide a significant boost to our economy. But it will not happen unless we make it happen. If Michigan's business and government leaders act boldly and decisively, we have a good chance to grab an important share of the future biofuels economy. However, if we don't step up, other states and other countries would be happy to leave us behind.

If we glance again at table 1.1, we can see some other sectors that would make good candidates for future economic growth, and some that probably would not. The service sector has been growing rapidly for decades, both in Michigan and in the rest of the country. Many people have an unfavorable impression of services, because some service-sector jobs pay low wages. (The stereotypical job involves flipping burgers at a fast-food restaurant.) However, we should remember that doctors, lawyers, and other highly paid professionals are also in the service sector. Services are likely to continue to grow. If Michigan can capture an increased share of the more highly skilled service jobs, it will be to our benefit.

One service industry that deserves special mention is health-care services. The health-care sector is likely to grow very rapidly in the next few decades. One reason for this is the aging of the population: The oldest Baby Boomers have reached their 60th birthdays. As this group gets older, the demand for health-care services is expected to keep growing. It is well known that doctors are among the most highly paid workers in the economy. Many nurses, medical technicians, and pharmacists are also well paid. If Michigan's medical centers were to expand their role as regional and national centers, it would be a boon for the economy.

The expansion of the health-care sector provides opportunities for growth in health-related manufacturing, as well as in services. The coming decades are likely to see substantial growth in the production of medical equipment, devices, and supplies. Michigan's economy will be stronger if we can gain a larger share of that booming sector. The chapter in *Michigan at the Millennium* by John Goddeeris of Michigan State University has a detailed discussion of health care in Michigan.

Another sector with growth potential is tourism. The Great Lakes and many smaller lakes provide Michigan with some of the most picturesque shorelines in the world. Michigan may not be able to rival Las Vegas or parts of Florida as a vacation spot, but it has the potential for growth as a regional tourism center. Of course, this will only happen if people are aware of Michigan's attractions. More aggressive marketing may be necessary to unlock the potential. For a discussion of travel, tourism, and recreation in Michigan, see the chapter in *Michigan at the Millennium* by Donald Holecek of Michigan State University.[7]

Realizing the Potential for Future Economic Growth

We have identified several sectors that have the potential to contribute greatly to the future growth of Michigan's economy. Many of these sectors involve advanced technologies. However, that growth potential will not be realized automatically. As Feinstein, Fulton, and Grimes put it in their *Michigan at the Millennium* chapter on high technology, "Success in the high-tech arena depends heavily on whether the state can supply an adequate pool of highly educated workers and sufficient venture capital."

In order to realize its potential for future economic growth, Michigan has to provide an environment in which businesses will decide to establish new operations in Michigan, and/or to expand existing operations. The process of providing that kind of environment is called "economic development." Michigan's economic-development efforts are discussed in *Michigan at the Millennium* by Timothy Bartik and George Erickcek of Kalamazoo's Upjohn Institute for Employment Research, and Peter Eisinger of Wayne State University. Bartik, Eisinger, and Erickcek make clear that Michigan, like other states, has a very wide range of activities in this area. These include (1) tax reductions, (2) extra infrastructure, (3) assistance to businesses in dealing with regulations, and (4) job training.

Michigan's system of economic development has many positive aspects. However, as pointed out by Bartik, Eisinger, and Erickcek, there is plenty of room for improvement. For one thing, there is a tendency for political leaders to reshuffle the economic-development efforts every few years. Of course, each governor has a right to influence the direction of policy. The challenge is to do so in a way that preserves continuity. Bartik and his coauthors also suggest that Michigan's economic-development efforts should be subjected to periodic outside reviews, to ensure accountability. My sense of the economic-development picture in Michigan is that we do a lot of things right, but we need to do much more. Because of the long-term decline of manufacturing, Michigan needs an excellent economic-development system, and not merely one that is OK.

Before leaving this topic, it is appropriate to comment on the role of taxes (especially business taxes) in economic development. In fact, Michigan has already cut taxes very significantly in the last few decades. Bartik et al. point out that Michigan is more aggressive than other states in using incentives to reduce business taxes. When a business makes a location decision, it must take many considerations into account. Businesses need a labor force with the appropriate skills. They need good labor-management relations. They need access to natural resources, and to a customer base. They need transportation and communications infrastructure. They need communities that provide a decent quality of life, with recreational, cultural, and educational opportunities. All of these things are at least as important as taxes, and most are far more important than taxes. If low taxes were the only consideration in business-location decisions, the entire U.S. economy would be located in Alabama. Actually, if low taxes were the only consideration in business-location decisions, there would not be any U.S. economy, because everything would have moved to the Bahamas and other tax-haven countries.

I put a skilled labor force at the beginning of my list of the influences on business-location decisions. I will say more about skills in chapter 2 of this book, and I will say more about taxes in chapter 5. For now, I want to emphasize that if we reduce taxes even more, it will of course be necessary to make even more reductions in public services. In recent years, Michigan has slashed taxes and slashed education budgets. This is penny-wise and pound-foolish in the extreme. As this book is being written, an effort is underway to eliminate Michigan's Single Business Tax (SBT). For reasons that I will outline in chapter 5, I am in favor of eliminating the SBT, *but only if we replace the revenues fully.* If we do not replace the revenues, we will almost certainly have to make more cuts to educational programs. In these days, when a highly skilled work force is so important, that would be a huge step in the wrong direction.

Employment and Unemployment in Michigan

In November 2005, about 5,102,000 Michigan residents were in the labor force. More than 4,768,000 were employed, while about 334,000 were unemployed.[8] That works out to an unemployment rate of 6.5 percent. At the same time, the national unemployment rate was 5.0 percent. Thus, in the fall of 2005, the Michigan economy would have needed about 80,000 additional jobs in order to bring Michigan's unemployment rate into line with the national average. Michigan's unemployment rate was the fifth highest among the 50 states.[9] (At the other end of the spectrum, Hawaii had the lowest unemployment rate in the United States in November 2005, at 2.7 percent.)

Just as there is variation among the unemployment rates of the 50 states, there is also variation among the regions within each state. The Labor Department calculates unemployment rates for 14 metropolitan areas in Michigan. In November 2005, these ranged from a low of 3.8 percent in Ann Arbor to a high of 6.8 percent in Flint. This is probably not a surprise. In part because of the University of Michigan, the region of Ann Arbor and Washtenaw County has a highly skilled labor force. On the other hand, Flint and Genesee County have suffered disproportionately from the shrinkage of the automobile industry. In *Michigan at the Millennium*, Richard Block and Dale Belman provide a fascinating discussion of the reasons why Flint bore such a large portion of the decline: The degree of tension between labor and management appears to have been higher in Flint than in other places. When General Motors had to close some plants, the place with the most contentious labor-management relations was a prime candidate.

Trends in Employment and Unemployment

In figure 1.3, we compare the unemployment trends for Michigan with those for the United States as a whole. This graph has several important stories to tell. First, figure 1.3 provides some perspective on the current situation in Michigan. Even though the Michigan unemployment rate is higher today than anyone would wish, it is far lower than it was in November 1982. At that time, the U.S. unemployment rate reached its highest level since the Great Depression, at 10.8 percent, and the unemployment rate in Michigan also reached its highest level since the Great Depression, at *16.9 percent*. In the fall of 1982, about 720,000 Michigan residents were unemployed. That is more than twice as many as are unemployed today. I do not mean to suggest that the people of Michigan should be happy with today's employment situation. However, it should be clear that we have weathered far worse. In fact, during the two decades from the recession of 1974–75 until the end of 1993, the unemployment rate in Michigan was *never* as low as it was in November 2005.

The theme of the previous paragraph has been, "It could be worse." However, the knowledge that things could be worse probably does not provide a great deal of comfort. No matter how we look at it, we cannot hide from the fact that Michigan's employment situation has been weak in recent years. At the end of 2005, the number of people working in Michigan was about the same as it had been at the end of 1997. Moreover, the number of people employed in Michigan at the end of 2005 was about 200,000 fewer than it had been when employment peaked in early 2000.

FIGURE 1.3 Unemployment Rates in Michigan and the United States, 1970–2004

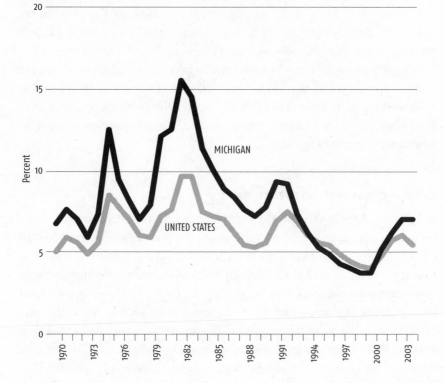

The most recent economic cycle in Michigan has not been as *severe* as the downturn of the early 1980s, but it has been *longer*. In the words of George Fulton and Donald Grimes, "What is so unusual about the labor market in Michigan recently is not the severity of the job losses, but the lack of a rebound. It's not that our current winter has been colder than usual; it's just that it never ends."[10]

The second story of figure 1.3 is that the unemployment rate in Michigan has a strong tendency to move in the same direction as the unemployment rate in the rest of the country. Good times for the rest of the United States tend to be good for Michigan. But when a recession leads to higher unemployment in the nation as a whole, Michigan suffers. This reminds us that Michigan's economy is intimately interconnected with the rest of the country. For better or worse, it is very difficult to separate Michigan's fortunes from those of the rest of the nation.

The third story told by figure 1.3 is that for much of this period, the Michigan economy was more volatile than the national economy. For example, from 1973 to 1975, a recession pushed the national unemployment rate up by 3.6 percentage points, from 4.9 percent to 8.5 percent. At the same time, Michigan's unemployment rate rose by 6.6 percentage points, from 5.9 percent to 12.5 percent.

Why has the roller coaster of the business cycle had steeper ups and downs for Michigan than for many other parts of the country? A big part of the answer lies in Michigan's heavy dependence on durable-goods manufacturing. The durable-goods sector produces "big-ticket items," such as automobiles and appliances. Consumers tend to postpone purchases of durable goods during hard times. Thus, the durable-goods industries are often hit hard during recessions. On the other hand, there is often a surge in orders for durable goods during an economic recovery. Thus, durable-goods manufacturing tends to have larger cycles than most other sectors of the economy. However, because of the decrease in the relative importance of durable-goods manufacturing, it appears that Michigan is not as cyclically sensitive as it once was.

The final story told by figure 1.3 begins in the 1990s. Michigan's unemployment rate had been higher than the national average for decades. But as the economic boom of the 1990s took hold, the Michigan economy experienced strong growth. From 1994 to 2000, the unemployment rate in Michigan was *lower* than the national unemployment rate. Even now, Michigan's unemployment rate does not exceed the national rate by the same large margins that sometimes existed in the 1970s and 1980s. In a chapter of *Michigan at the Millennium*, George Johnson of the University of Michigan suggests that this is an expected consequence of the decline in the Michigan wage rates, relative to the national average.

Incomes in Michigan: Levels and Trends

Figure 1.4 shows the growth of per capita personal income in Michigan since 1950. This graph shows "real" (inflation-adjusted) income: all of the values in figure 1.4 have been converted to 2004 dollars.[11]

In Michigan, income per person was nearly three times as large in 2004 as it had been in 1950, even after adjusting for inflation. However, figure 1.4 also shows that this overall pattern of rising income has not been smooth over time: not surprisingly, income per person has decreased during recessions.

The rate of income growth was slower in the second half of the period shown in figure 1.4 than in the first half. Incomes in Michigan grew by about 98 percent in the 27-year period from 1950 to 1977, but only by about 46 percent in the 27-year period from 1977 to 2004.

Comparing Incomes in Michigan with Incomes in the Rest of the United States

Table 1.2 shows per capita personal income for the 50 states and the District of Columbia for 2004. In that year, incomes in Michigan ranked 21st among the 50 states, or 22nd if we include the District of Columbia. Michigan's per capita income of just over $32,000 was about 3 percent below the national average.[12]

Table 1.2 shows the situation for a single year. Figure 1.5 shows the trend over time in the relationship between per capita personal incomes in Michigan and those in the United States as a whole, from 1950 to 2004.

Figure 1.5 shows that income per person was persistently higher in Michigan than in the rest of the country until the early 1980s. In several years in the 1950s and 1960s, Michigan incomes were more than 10 percent above the national average. However, the deep recession of the early 1980s was especially hard on Michigan. Incomes in the state fell substantially relative to the national average. Since then, the level of income in Michigan has most often been below the national average.[13]

It is useful to compare figure 1.4 with figure 1.5. In figure 1.4, we can see the good news that incomes in Michigan have grown. But figure 1.5 shows the bad news that income growth has been slower in Michigan than in the rest of the country.

Figure 1.5 includes the trend line that provides the best fit for the data. The trend line shows that, relative to the national average level of income, Michigan lost about one percentage point every three years. If this trend were to continue for another few decades, Michigan's relative standing would be similar to that occupied by Arkansas and Mississippi today.

Figure 1.5 shows that *incomes in Michigan have been declining relative to the U.S. average for a very long time.* This is a crucial point, because long-term problems

FIGURE 1.4 Real Per-Capita Personal Income in Michigan, 1950–2004 (in 2004 Dollars)

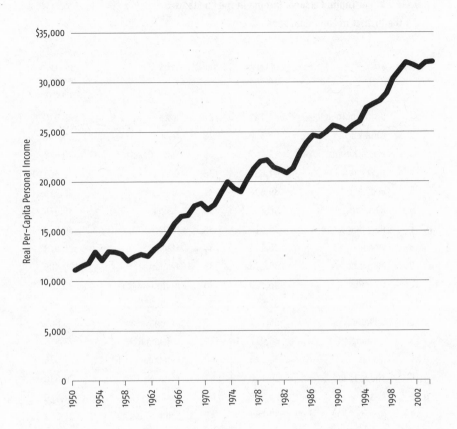

require long-term solutions. Of course, policies focused on the short term can make a difference, and sometimes short-term policies can make a big difference. However, there are no quick fixes to the fundamental economic problems facing the people of Michigan. If we think in terms of quick fixes rather than long-run strategies, the results are likely to be disappointing.

The Rise in Income Inequality

In the previous section, we saw that the economy of Michigan has experienced income growth over the last few decades (although at a slower pace

TABLE 1.2 Per Capita Personal Income in the 50 States
and the District of Columbia, 2004

RANK	STATE	PER CAPITA PERSONAL INCOME	RANK	STATE	PER CAPITA PERSONAL INCOME
1	District of Columbia	$52,101	27	Iowa	$30,970
2	Connecticut	45,506	28	Texas	30,697
3	Massachusetts	42,102	29	South Dakota	30,617
4	New Jersey	41,636	30	Oregon	30,584
5	Maryland	39,629	31	Missouri	30,516
6	New York	38,333	32	Georgia	30,074
7	New Hampshire	36,676	33	Indiana	30,070
8	Virginia	36,175	34	Maine	29,973
9	Minnesota	36,173	35	Tennessee	29,806
10	Colorado	36,109	36	North Carolina	29,303
11	Delaware	35,559	37	North Dakota	29,247
12	California	35,172	38	Arizona	28,609
13	Washington	35,017	39	Oklahoma	27,819
14	Illinois	34,725	40	Montana	27,666
15	Rhode Island	34,180	41	Alabama	27,630
16	Alaska	34,085	42	Louisiana	27,219
17	Nevada	33,783	43	South Carolina	27,153
18	Pennsylvania	33,257	44	Kentucky	27,151
19	Hawaii	32,606	45	Utah	26,946
20	Nebraska	32,276	46	Idaho	26,839
21	Wisconsin	32,063	47	New Mexico	26,154
22	**Michigan**	**32,052**	48	Arkansas	25,724
23	Vermont	31,737	49	West Virginia	25,681
24	Florida	31,460	50	Mississippi	24,379
25	Ohio	31,135	51	Wyoming	24,199
26	Kansas	31,003		**U.S. Average**	**$33,041**

Source: United States Department of Commerce, Bureau of Economic Analysis; http://www.bea.gov/bea/regional/spi/drill.cfm.

FIGURE 1.5 Real Per-Capita Personal Income: Michigan as a Percentage of the United States, 1950–2004

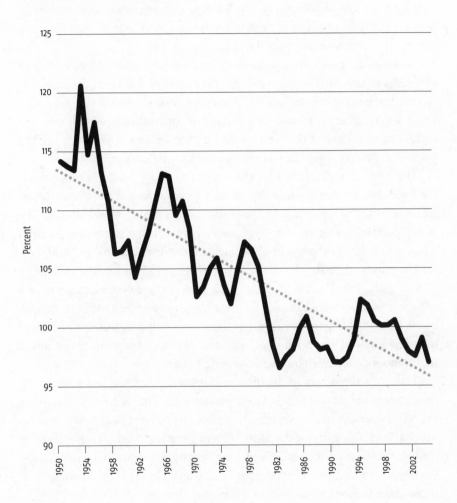

than the rest of the country). However, growth in *average* income does not necessarily translate into income growth for *everyone*. In fact, since about 1975, the degree of inequality in the United States has increased tremendously. In 1975, the most affluent 20 percent of U.S. households received about 43.6 percent of the income in the country, according to census data.[14] By 2004, the income share of the top 20 percent of households had risen to 50.1 percent. Over the same time period, the income share of the top five percent of households rose from 16.5 percent to 21.8 percent. In Michigan, and in the rest of the United States, income inequality has risen to levels that have not been seen since the early part of the twentieth century.

This is a massive shift, and it is one of the most important economic stories of the last generation. Here is one way to get a sense of the size of the change: if income had been distributed across the income classes in 2004 in the same way that it was distributed in 1975, the 5 percent of American households with the highest incomes would be receiving about $500 *billion* less per year, and the poorest 95 percent would be receiving about $500 billion more per year.

There are several reasons for the increasing concentration of income in the hands of the most affluent. The most important reason has to do with an increase in the wage premium for workers with higher levels of skill. The wages of college-educated workers have increased strongly in recent decades, while the wages of other groups have stagnated or even shrunk. In *Michigan at the Millennium*, these trends are discussed by Rebecca Blank of the University of Michigan. She shows that the median weekly wage of Michigan workers with at least a bachelor's degree increased by nearly 30 percent from 1979 to 2000, after adjusting for inflation. For those with only a high-school diploma, inflation-adjusted wages fell by 8.5 percent. The wages of workers without a high-school diploma fell by an astonishing 25 percent.

Thus, it is important to qualify the statements that one hears about the poor performance of the Michigan economy. The economy has been mediocre overall, but it has not been mediocre for everyone. The last generation has been fabulous for the most affluent people in Michigan. For those at the top, there has been unprecedented prosperity. For those in the middle, the Michigan economy of recent decades has been lackluster at best. For many of those at the bottom, it has been an economic disaster.

The increase in inequality has two very important implications. First, the rising wage premium for a college education tells us that the future belongs to the educated, now more than ever. Unfortunately, as we shall see in the next chapter, Michigan lags behind the national average in terms of educational attainment.

The second implication of the increase in inequality has to do with who pays taxes in Michigan. Now, more than ever, those at the top have greater ability to pay taxes. On that basis, one might expect that tax policies in Michigan would have changed, to cushion the blow to those at the bottom of the income scale. However, just the opposite has occurred. Ironically, as a result of the tax-policy changes in Michigan in the last 12 years, the percentage of income paid in state and local taxes has increased for the poorest Michigan residents. On the other hand, those at the top of the income distribution have benefited from substantial reductions in taxes. In chapter 5 of this book, I will discuss tax policy in considerable detail.

The Importance of Trade with the Rest of the United States

During the first few years after America won its independence from Great Britain, the 13 former colonies had the authority to use tariffs to interfere with trade across state lines. The leaders who wrote the U.S. Constitution in 1787 recognized that these tariffs were harming the national economy. In Article I, Sections 8 and 10, the Constitution enshrined the principle that Congress (rather than the individual states) has the responsibility to regulate interstate commerce. Thus, today, when a Michigan company sells to customers in Ohio, it is not necessary to pay tariffs. In effect, the Constitution created a nation that would eventually become the world's largest free-trade zone. This has contributed immeasurably to American economic growth.

Michigan's economy is very closely interconnected with the economy of the rest of the United States. The positive aspect of these close connections is that the people of Michigan are much more affluent than they would be if they were completely on their own. (If Michigan were "self-sufficient," Michigan residents would be restricted to consuming things that are made in Michigan. There would be no fresh vegetables in winter, and few citrus fruits at any time of year. There would be very little gasoline. And, if the state were cut off from the rest of the country, Michigan residents would not be able to sell cars, office furniture, or breakfast cereal to people in other states.)

Overall, Michigan gains tremendously from being able to trade freely with the rest of the country. At the same time, however, since the Michigan economy depends so much on connections with the rest of the United States, the people of Michigan have only a limited ability to control the Michigan economy. Most people probably yearn to be the masters of their own destiny, but the fact is that Michigan's economic situation is greatly affected by things that happen far beyond Michigan's borders.

This does not mean that the people of Michigan are completely helpless. In fact, much of this book will be devoted to discussions of policy options for Michigan. However, it is important to keep things in perspective. It would be nice if someone could snap his or her fingers and create 100,000 new high-paying jobs. In fact, however, there are no easy solutions to difficult problems. Neither the governor, nor the legislature, nor anyone else can produce a dramatic transformation of the Michigan economy in the short term. The future holds positive prospects, but they will take time to achieve.

Michigan's Geographic Isolation

I have emphasized that connections with the rest of the U.S. economy are vitally important for Michigan's prosperity. However, Michigan is not as connected to the rest of the country as it might be, because of accidents of geography. The Great Lakes are a wonderful asset for Michigan, but they place physical barriers between Michigan and the rest of the country. Whereas states like Missouri and Tennessee are completely surrounded by other states, much of the outline of Michigan does not have a direct land connection to other states. In only three states (Alaska, Hawaii, and Maine) does a smaller percentage of the state's outline involve a land border with other states than it does in Michigan.

This relative isolation has an important effect on the distribution of economic activity in Michigan. It means that an economic advantage is enjoyed by the parts of Michigan that are closer to the rest of the country. This is one of the reasons why more than 80 percent of Michigan's population, and more than 90 percent of its economy, are within 100 miles of the southern borders with Indiana and Ohio.[15]

Regional Income Differences in Michigan

As suggested in the previous paragraph, there are big differences in the level of economic activity among the regions of Michigan. Table 1.3 reveals striking regional disparities in the level of per capita income for Michigan counties in 2003. The per capita incomes for individual counties range from more than

$49,000 in Oakland County to less than $17,000 in Oscoda County. Thus, the most affluent parts of Michigan are among the most affluent places in the world. However, the poorest Michigan counties have income levels that are somewhat higher than Greece or South Korea, but lower than Spain.

Table 1.3 shows that Oakland County is by far the most affluent county in Michigan. The table also reveals that the affluence of Oakland County is part of a broader pattern. The regions with the highest incomes in Michigan are mostly in the southern Lower Peninsula, and especially in southeastern Lower Michigan. The four counties with the highest per capita incomes are all in the region served by the Southeast Michigan Council of Governments (SEMCOG).[16] All seven of the SEMCOG counties rank among the 14 counties with the highest incomes, out of the 83 counties in Michigan. As a result, the SEMCOG counties have about 56 percent of the personal income in Michigan, even though they include only about 48 percent of the population. Sixteen of the 20 highest-income counties in Michigan are in the southern Lower Peninsula.[17]

All of the major metropolitan areas in Michigan are in the southern half of the Lower Peninsula. Thus, when we say that the most affluent counties in Michigan tend to be in the southern Lower Peninsula, it is almost the same as saying that the most affluent counties are in metropolitan areas. For the last several decades, the per capita incomes in Michigan's metropolitan counties have been about one-third larger, on average, than the per capita incomes in the nonmetropolitan counties. Not a single one of the 42 counties with the lowest per capita incomes in Michigan is in a metropolitan area.

The Importance of Trade with the Rest of the World

In the previous section, we discussed the effect of Michigan's geographical isolation from the rest of the United States. This presents a challenge in that it is difficult for some parts of Michigan to maintain economic connections with the rest of the country. It also presents an opportunity, because it is important to take advantage of the connections that we *do* have. Our relationships with the rest of the world, beyond the borders of the United States, present similar challenges and opportunities. Once again, geography plays an important role. In particular, Michigan is one of the leading gateways to

TABLE 1.3 Per Capita Incomes in 2003, for Michigan's 83 Counties

RANK	COUNTY	INCOME PER PERSON	RANK	COUNTY	INCOME PER PERSON
1	Oakland	$49,048	22	Dickinson	$27,727
2	Washtenaw	$38,323	23	Berrien	$27,572
3	Livingston	$35,869	24	Genesee	$27,521
4	Macomb	$34,206	25	Calhoun	$26,778
5	Midland	$32,821	26	Bay	$26,726
6	Leelanau	$31,599	27	Saginaw	$26,454
7	Kent	$30,624	28	Cass	$26,429
8	Emmet	$30,467	29	Allegan	$26,190
9	Kalamazoo	$30,429	30	Huron	$26,175
10	Monroe	$29,914	31	Antrim	$26,042
11	Wayne	$29,879	32	Jackson	$25,712
12	Grand Traverse	$29,662	33	Mackinac	$25,663
13	Ingham	$28,825	34	Alpena	$24,814
14	St. Clair	$28,646	35	Sanilac	$24,811
15	Ottawa	$28,570	36	Benzie	$24,747
16	Charlevoix	$28,506	37	Delta	$24,704
17	Clinton	$28,464	38	St. Joseph	$24,496
18	Lenawee	$28,452	39	Muskegon	$24,468
19	Eaton	$28,399	40	Otsego	$24,465
20	Barry	$28,153	41	Van Buren	$24,362
21	Lapeer	$27,928	42	Marquette	$24,191

Source: http://www.bea.gov/bea/regional/reis/.

Ontario, the economic heartland of Canada. Trade with Canada is one of the central pillars of Michigan's economy.

Michigan has the *eighth* largest economy of the 50 states, but we are the *fourth* largest exporting state. Thus, more than most states, Michigan has a lot to lose from excessive interference with international trade, and a lot to gain from trade improvements. *Michigan at the Millennium* includes an

RANK	COUNTY	INCOME PER PERSON	RANK	COUNTY	INCOME PER PERSON
43	Mason	$24,117	65	Gogebic	$20,985
44	Shiawassee	$24,020	66	Osceola	$20,947
45	Hillsdale	$23,742	67	Roscommon	$20,872
46	Cheboygan	$22,995	68	Houghton	$20,747
47	Iron	$22,822	69	Iosco	$20,740
48	Wexford	$22,781	70	Montcalm	$20,604
49	Manistee	$22,775	71	Clare	$20,523
50	Menominee	$22,558	72	Lake	$20,246
51	Keweenaw	$22,422	73	Crawford	$20,135
52	Ionia	$22,319	74	Mecosta	$20,049
53	Branch	$22,318	75	Chippewa	$19,682
54	Gratiot	$22,287	76	Ogemaw	$19,662
55	Ontonagon	$22,264	77	Alger	$19,648
56	Newaygo	$22,123	78	Montmorency	$19,641
57	Isabella	$22,111	79	Baraga	$19,229
58	Oceana	$21,995	80	Missaukee	$19,043
59	Tuscola	$21,985	81	Kalkaska	$18,881
60	Schoolcraft	$21,899	82	Luce	$18,829
61	Arenac	$21,655	83	Oscoda	$16,674
62	Presque Isle	$21,454			
63	Gladwin	$21,263		**Median County**	**$24,191**
64	Alcona	$21,109		**Statewide Average**	**$31,178**

excellent discussion of international issues by Alan Deardorff of the University of Michigan.

In the United States, the federal government determines international trade policies. Thus, Michigan's governor and legislature have relatively little control over international trade policy. Nevertheless, it makes sense to comment on some issues of international trade policy, for two reasons. First, the issues are of crucial importance to Michigan. Second, the public debate on trade is often marked by confusion and misunderstanding.[18]

American economic history includes many cases of interference with international trade. The most notorious of these was the Smoot-Hawley Tariff Act of 1930, which raised tariffs to their highest levels in history. The Smoot-Hawley tariffs helped to accelerate the downward spiral of worldwide economic activity that became the Great Depression. Fortunately, world leaders recognized the damage done by the high tariffs of the 1930s. Since the Second World War, the United States has participated in a long series of negotiations for mutual tariff reduction. (The most famous of these was the "Kennedy Round," sponsored by President John F. Kennedy.) The reduced obstacles to international trade have helped to fuel the worldwide economic prosperity of the last 60 years.

Of course, this does not mean that international trade has no problems. Some individual businesses and individual workers have been harmed by competition from abroad. The question is: What is the best way to help these workers and businesses? There is general agreement in the economics profession that large trade barriers are not the best way. Instead, it makes sense to embrace international trade (because it increases the overall standard of living), and to provide targeted assistance to those who have been harmed by trade.

The reasoning used here, in relation to international trade, is similar to the reasoning used earlier in this chapter, in relation to the transitions out of agriculture and manufacturing. The improvements in agricultural productivity contributed greatly to the overall standard of living, but they also forced a transition that was difficult for some farm workers. The improvements in manufacturing productivity have contributed greatly to the overall standard of living, but they have also forced a transition that has been difficult for some factory workers. Similarly, international trade contributes greatly to the overall level of prosperity, but it can lead to difficult adjustments for some workers. In each case, the consensus in the economics profession is that it is good to embrace the mechanisms that create general economic prosperity, but also to provide assistance (such as unemployment insurance and retraining programs) to those who are adversely affected.

Of course, because of security concerns, international trade must not be completely unfettered. The challenge is to achieve the greatest possible economic benefit from international trade while preserving security. In the aftermath of the events of September 11, 2001, heightened security led to considerable congestion at border crossings. Some of the congestion was relieved by the opening of new U.S. Customs booths on the Detroit side of the Ambassador Bridge in 2004. Nevertheless, eventually, it will almost certainly be necessary to build a new bridge or tunnel in the Detroit area. When producers in Ontario want to ship goods to the eastern third of the United States, they have a choice of sending the goods through border crossings in Detroit or Port Huron, or through crossings in the region of Buffalo–Niagara Falls, New York. For the sake of the future economic health of Michigan, it makes sense to ensure that the Michigan border crossings are modern, fast, and efficient.

Conclusion

In this chapter, we have taken a whirlwind tour of the Michigan economy. Here are some of the highlights:

- Manufacturing accounts for a much larger share of the economy in Michigan than in the rest of the United States. In 2003, manufacturing was nearly 21 percent of the Michigan economy, but only about 13 percent of the U.S. economy.
- As a fraction of the overall economy, the manufacturing sector has been declining in relative importance for decades, both in Michigan and in the rest of the United States. Many of the challenges facing Michigan today are due to the fact that the Michigan economy is heavily involved in a sector that is in relative decline.
- In the 1970s, 1980s, and early 1990s, the unemployment rate in Michigan was persistently higher than the unemployment rate for the United States as a whole. However, the Michigan unemployment rate fell below the U.S. rate in the late 1990s. This is partly due to the relative decline in Michigan wage rates. In the early years of the twenty-first century, Michigan's unemployment rate has again been higher than the national rate, although it is still far lower than it was in much of the 1970s and 1980s. Nevertheless, the recovery from the 2001 recession has been very slow in Michigan. In late 2005, the number of employed people in Michigan was about the same as it had been eight years earlier.

- Unemployment in Michigan tends to rise when national unemployment is rising, and fall when national unemployment is falling. In addition, heavy dependence on durable-goods manufacturing has historically made the economy more cyclical in Michigan than in the rest of the United States, with larger upward and downward swings in the unemployment rate. However, Michigan's economy is probably not as volatile as it once was.

- Per capita income in Michigan nearly tripled from 1950 to 2004, even after adjusting for inflation. However, the income growth was slower in Michigan than in the United States as a whole. Until the early 1980s, per capita incomes in Michigan were substantially higher than the national average. Since then, however, Michigan's incomes have been slightly below the national average in most years. Over the last 55 years, the ratio of per capita income in Michigan to per capita income in the United States as a whole has decreased by more than 15 percent.

- All across the United States, the distribution of income has become much more unequal since the 1970s. Thus, although the overall level of income has grown in the past few decades, the households at the top of the income distribution have received most of the gains. Many people at the bottom of the income distribution have suffered a decrease in their standard of living.

- The Great Lakes are a magnificent natural resource. However, in this era when land-based transportation is far more prevalent than lake-based transportation, much of Michigan is geographically isolated. The major land connections with the rest of the United States and with Ontario are concentrated in the southern Lower Peninsula. The population and the economy of Michigan are both dominated by southern (and especially southeastern) Lower Michigan. Per capita incomes are much higher in the southern part of the state. The southern Lower Peninsula accounts for more than 80 percent of Michigan's population, and more than 90 percent of its income.

- Michigan is one of the leading gateways between Canada and the United States. As a result, Michigan is one of the nation's leaders for international exports. Maintaining international connections, especially with Canada, is important for Michigan's economic future.

We have now analyzed some of the central facts and trends of Michigan's economy. In the next chapter, we take a closer look at Michigan's human resources. The skills of our people have played a huge role in the past, and they are likely to be even more crucial in the knowledge-driven economy of the future.

NOTES

1. The Bureau of Economic Analysis (BEA, a branch of the U.S. Commerce Department) provides statistics for the value of production in various industries, for the 50 states and the District of Columbia. The BEA data are available in great detail at *http://www .bea.gov/bea/regional/gsp/*.

2. For the United States as a whole, the trend for manufacturing is almost continuously downward. For Michigan, the overall trend is downward, but there are some noticeable short-term upturns. In fact, it is common for regional economies to be more volatile than the national economy. By definition, the U.S. economy is the weighted average of the economies of all of the states; the fluctuations in the individual states tend to even out when we combine them into a national average.

3. For a discussion of the southward trend in automobile production in the United States, see Kim Hill and Emilio Brahmst, "The Auto Industry Moving South: An Examination of Trends," available on the website of the Center for Automotive Research, at *http://www .cargroup.org/pdfs/North-SouthPaper.pdf*.

4. The data shown in figure 1.2 are from the website of *Automotive News*, at *https://www .autonews.com/*, and from the American Automobile Manufacturers' Association, at *http:// www.economagic.com/aama.htm*. The Big Three have done relatively better in the truck market than in the car market. Still, figure 1.2 paints an ugly picture for the American auto companies.

5. These data come from table 3 of "Michigan's Industrial Structure and Competitive Advantage: How Did We Get Into This Pickle and Where Do We Go From Here?" by George A. Fulton and Donald R. Grimes. The Fulton-Grimes paper was prepared for "Where Do We Go From Here?"—a conference held in Ann Arbor on March 14, 2006. The paper is available at *http://closup.umich.edu/research/conferences/wdwgfh/wdwgfh-papers.html*. According to Fulton and Grimes, "Some of this differential arises from a much higher concentration of skilled-trade workers in Michigan . . . The chief difference, though, is the higher wages that have been negotiated by unions in the state."

6. In addition to requiring fewer workers, agriculture now requires less land. At one time, about 19 million acres of land in Michigan were used for agricultural purposes, out of a total of about 35 million acres. Nowadays, however, agriculture accounts for only about 10 million acres. In other words, about one-fourth of the land in Michigan has reverted from agriculture to its original condition, or been adapted to other uses. Much of this land is marginally productive land in the northern Lower Peninsula, which has now returned to forest. For a discussion, see chapter 10 of *Michigan at the Millennium* by Arlen Leholm, Raymond Vlasin, and John Ferris of Michigan State University.

7. Table 1.1 also shows a few sectors that are *not* likely to be major engines of economic growth for Michigan in the near future. Unless a major new oil field is discovered, the mining sector in Michigan probably will not reach the level of importance that it enjoys in some other parts of the country. Also, at a time when military bases are being closed, it seems unlikely that Michigan can count on a surge in military-related economic activity.

8. The data on employment and unemployment for states and metropolitan areas can be found at the website of the Bureau of Labor Statistics, at *http://stats.bls.gov/lau/home.htm.*

9. The two states with the highest unemployment rates in the fall of 2005 were Louisiana and Mississippi, which were still recovering from the effects of Hurricane Katrina.

10. Fulton and Grimes, "Michigan's Industrial Structure and Competitive Advantage," 5.

11. The income data for states are from the Bureau of Economic Analysis of the U.S. Department of Commerce. The data are available at *http://www.bea.gov/bea/regional/statelocal.htm.* The adjustment for inflation is based on the Personal Consumption Expenditures deflator, which is also calculated by the Bureau of Economic Analysis. These data are available in table 1.1.4, "Price Indexes for Gross Domestic Product," at *http://www.bea.gov/ bea/dn/nipaweb/SelectTable.asp?Selected=N.*

12. Thus, Michigan's incomes are higher than those of the *median* state, but lower than the national *average*. In fact, only 17 states and the District of Columbia are above the national average. This is because the national average is weighted by population, and four of the six most-populous states are in the top 17 when we rank by income.

13. From the 1950s to the 1970s, per capita personal income in Michigan often ranked about 11th or 12th among the 50 states. In 1973, Michigan ranked 8th. However, since 1990, Michigan has usually ranked about 20th.

14. See Carmen DeNavas-Walt, Bernadette D. Proctor, and Cheryl Hill Lee, U.S. Census Bureau, Current Population Reports, P60–229, *Income, Poverty, and Health Insurance Coverage in the United States: 2004* (Washington, D.C.: U.S. Government Printing Office, 2005). This report is available at *http://www.census.gov/prod/2005pubs/p60–229.pdf.* For the income share

of the top 20 percent of households, see table A-3, "Selected Measures of Household Income Dispersion: 1967 to 2004."

15. Of course, the Great Lakes offer opportunities for *waterborne* commerce, even though they form a barrier to *land* connections. However, in today's economy, the vast majority of commercial transportation is by land. This is discussed in the chapter on transportation in *Michigan at the Millennium* by Kenneth Boyer of Michigan State University. Boyer reports that more than three-fourths of the value of Michigan freight originations are by truck. It is possible that there could be a resurgence of shipping on the Great Lakes at some point in the future. For now, however, the land highways are king, and this provides an economic advantage for the southern Lower Peninsula relative to the rest of Michigan.

16. SEMCOG includes the following counties: Livingston, Macomb, Monroe, Oakland, St. Clair, Washtenaw, and Wayne.

17. The other four are all in parts of the northern Lower Peninsula that thrive on recreation and tourism. For a discussion, see Donald Holecek's chapter in *Michigan at the Millennium*.

18. Trade deficits are the subject of an especially high degree of confusion. Currently, the United States is running very large trade deficits. (In other words, the total value of our exports is less than the total value of our imports.) It is sometimes suggested that trade policies are to blame. At best, however, that is a very incomplete explanation. The facts are that the federal government is running very large budget deficits, and that American households save very little. Consequently, as a nation, we are consuming more than we produce. When a household spends more than it makes, it has to borrow. The same is true for a nation. When the United States spends more than it makes, it has to borrow from other countries. Given our large budget deficits and our low savings rate, the only way to maintain investment in the American economy is for much of the financing to come from abroad. The trade deficits are mainly driven by America's consumption binge, and not by anyone's trade policies.

Michigan's Human Resources

Michigan's greatest asset is its people. In this chapter, we consider the population, labor force, and educational system in Michigan. We begin with a brief look at the trends in population. For a much more detailed discussion of Michigan demographics, see the chapter in *Michigan at the Millennium* by the state demographer, Kenneth Darga.

Population Trends in Michigan

In 2004, Michigan had a population of about 10.1 million. This is about 3.4 percent of the population of the United States, and it makes Michigan the eighth-most-populous state. Table 2.1 provides some perspective by showing the 20 states with the largest populations.[1]

In 1900, Michigan's population was about 2.4 million. Thus, the population increased about fourfold during the twentieth century. However, the rate of growth has been uneven over time. Figure 2.1 shows that Michigan's population grew very rapidly from 1910 to 1930. The growth slowed down in the Depression decade of the 1930s, both for Michigan and for the rest of the United States. However, Michigan once again experienced rapid population growth from 1940 to 1970. Michigan's manufacturing-based economy was

TABLE 2.1 Population of the Twenty Largest States, 2004

RANK	STATE	POPULATION (IN MILLIONS)	RANK	STATE	POPULATION (IN MILLIONS)
1	California	35.8	12	Virginia	7.5
2	Texas	22.5	13	Massachusetts	6.4
3	New York	19.3	14	Indiana	6.2
4	Florida	17.4	15	Washington	6.2
5	Illinois	12.7	16	Tennessee	5.9
6	Pennsylvania	12.4	17	Missouri	5.8
7	Ohio	11.5	18	Arizona	5.7
8	**Michigan**	**10.1**	19	Maryland	5.6
9	Georgia	8.9	20	Wisconsin	5.5
10	New Jersey	8.7			
11	North Carolina	8.5		**United States**	**293.7**

Source: United States Bureau of the Census; http://www.census.gov/popest/states/tables/NST-EST2005-01.xls.

booming in the middle decades of the twentieth century, and this was associated with rapid population growth.

Since 1970, however, the growth rate of Michigan's population has fallen dramatically. In the 30-year period from 1940 to 1970, the state's population grew by about 69 percent. In the next 30 years, from 1970 to 2000, the population grew by only 12 percent. If Michigan's population had grown as rapidly after 1970 as it grew in the 30 years before 1970, it would be more than 15 million, instead of the 10 million who actually live in the state today!

As a result of the slower growth since 1970, Michigan's share of the U.S. population has shrunk significantly, from 4.4 percent in 1970 to 3.4 percent now. The slower growth is partly a reflection of Michigan's sluggish economic performance in recent decades, which we have already discussed in chapter 1. It is also a reflection of the general movement of the U.S. population toward the south and west.[2]

There is one silver lining in the cloud of slower population growth. All else equal, a smaller population means less pressure on the environment.

FIGURE 2.1 Population in Michigan, 1900–2000

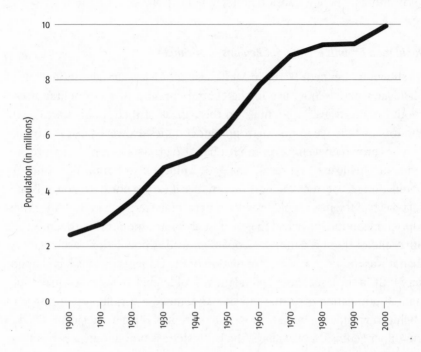

Michigan (especially the southern Lower Peninsula) has much more open space than it would have had if the rapid population growth of the mid-twentieth century had continued. We will return to issues of land use and the environment in the next chapter.

The Aging of the Michigan Population

In 1900, about 5 percent of Michigan's people were over 65 years of age. By 2004, the elderly population had increased to about 12.3 percent of the state's total population.[3] In Michigan, as in the rest of the United States, that percentage is expected to continue to increase. The Census Bureau estimates that the over-65 age group will rise to 16 percent of the Michigan population by 2020, and 19.5 percent by 2030.[4] Thus, the percentage of the population who are elderly will grow by about as much in the next 25 years as it grew in the last 100 years. As we shall see, the aging of the population has important implications for health-care policy, pension policy, and tax policy.

Population Growth in Different Regions in Michigan

As shown by Kenneth Darga in *Michigan at the Millennium,* about one-half of Michigan's people now live in the central counties of metropolitan areas, about one-third live in counties on the fringes of metropolitan areas, and about one-sixth live in nonmetropolitan counties. However, just as population has grown unevenly over time, it has also grown unevenly across the regions of Michigan. As a result, the geographical distribution of Michigan's population has been changing. In recent decades, the northern Lower Peninsula has had the most rapid growth in percentage terms, and the fringe metropolitan counties have had the greatest absolute amounts of growth. At the other end of the spectrum, the Upper Peninsula's population is smaller now than it was in 1910. Since the population of the Upper Peninsula has changed very little in the last century, while the rest of Michigan has experienced substantial population growth, the U.P. has claimed a shrinking percentage of Michigan's residents. In 1910, about 11.6 percent of Michigan residents lived in the Upper Peninsula. Nowadays, the U.P.'s share is only about 3.1 percent.

The Decline of the Central Cities

Figure 2.2 covers roughly the same time period as figure 2.1, but for the City of Detroit.[5] The meteoric rise and dizzying fall of Detroit's population are much more dramatic than the population trends for the entire state. Between 1900 and 1930, Detroit's population grew with astonishing speed. By 1930, the city had more than 1.5 million people, and more than 32 percent of Michigan residents were Detroiters. The city's population continued to grow in the 1930s and 1940s, although at a much slower pace. Detroit's population began to decline in the middle of the twentieth century. The city has lost more than half its population since 1950, and fewer than 9 percent of the people of Michigan are now residents of Detroit.

The racial composition of Detroit's population has changed in equally dramatic fashion. As recently as 1960, blacks accounted for about 29 percent of Detroit's population. Since then, the number of white residents of Detroit

FIGURE 2.2 Population of Detroit, 1900–2004

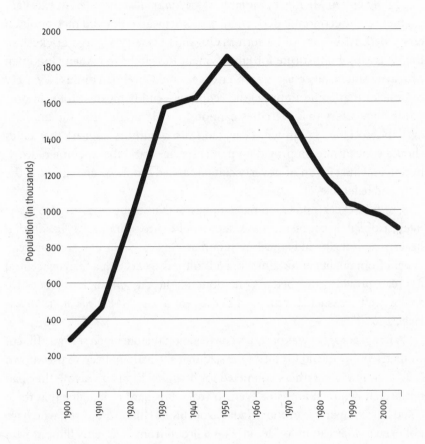

has decreased by more than one million. In 2000, 81.6 percent of Detroit's people were African American, and fewer than 13 percent were white. In his chapter in *Michigan at the Millennium*, Kenneth Darga documents the astonishing degree of racial segregation in the Detroit area. Darga's figure 3.22 shows an amazingly sharp division at the border between Detroit and its northern suburbs: virtually every census tract south of 8 Mile Road is more than 80 percent nonwhite, whereas virtually every tract north of 8 Mile Road is more than 80 percent white.

In 2004, the Detroit poverty rate of 33.6 percent was the highest in the nation, and nearly half of Detroit's children were in poverty.[6]

Detroit merits special attention because of its size, but it is not the only struggling city in Michigan. *Michigan at the Millennium* includes an excellent chapter on the economic performance of Michigan cities and metropolitan areas, by David Crary of Eastern Michigan University, George Erickcek of the W. E. Upjohn Institute for Employment Research, and Allen Goodman of Wayne State University.[7] Crary, Erickcek, and Goodman discuss a variety of policies that could improve the economies of Michigan's cities. Importantly, they stress that the cities cannot do it alone. Because the tax base available to cities is limited, Crary and his coauthors suggest that cities should concentrate on providing public services, and that income redistribution and alleviation of poverty can be carried out more effectively at the state and federal level.

Crary, Erickcek, and Goodman emphasize that strong cities are also in the interest of suburban residents. A successful metropolitan area "has both a healthy central city and a healthy suburban ring . . . Suburban residents can benefit from quality entertainment and cultural events that a thriving central city can provide, and better conditions in the city mean fewer negative spillover effects, such as crime, from the central city." (*Michigan at the Millennium*, 237).

A few years ago, I was part of a conversation that included several affluent women from Oakland County. One said that she had not been to downtown Detroit in 15 years. Others competed for bragging rights by saying they had not been downtown for 25 or even 30 years. It is hard to imagine that there could be a comparable group of ladies from Short Hills, New Jersey, who have not been to Manhattan for decades, or a group from Wilmette, Illinois, who have not been to downtown Chicago for decades. As long as it is a badge of honor for Detroit-area suburbanites to avoid downtown Detroit, it is a problem for all of Michigan, and not just for our largest city.

Michigan can never achieve its full potential while its largest city is racially isolated and economically depressed. For one thing, in the future the economy will increasingly be driven by talent and creativity. Creative people often congregate in vibrant cities. Right now, when a young and talented person looks for a vibrant city, he or she is probably much more likely to think of Chicago than Detroit. In recent years, Michigan's economy has suffered from the loss of tens of thousands of young people. A revitalized Detroit will help Michigan to retain these valuable human resources.

Parts of Detroit received a makeover in preparation for Super Bowl XL, which took place at Ford Field in February 2006. There are other encouraging signs of improvement along the riverfront and elsewhere, but much remains to be done.

The Michigan Labor Force

In this section, we take a brief look at some key characteristics of the labor force in Michigan. In the next section, we consider the educational attainment of the labor force, which is perhaps the most important characteristic of all. Because the labor market is so important, many chapters in *Michigan at the Millennium* deal with labor-force issues, and three chapters are especially noteworthy for their in-depth discussions of labor-related issues. George Johnson of the University of Michigan surveys the overall labor-market situation. Rebecca Blank, also of the University of Michigan, focuses on the low-wage, low-skill labor market. And Stephen Woodbury of Michigan State University considers unemployment insurance, workers' compensation, and reemployment programs.

Women in the Michigan Labor Force

Throughout the United States, the labor-force participation rate of women has been increasing for decades. The trend in Michigan is fairly similar to the trend in the United States as a whole. In 1976, about 39.5 percent of the workers in Michigan were female, compared with about 40.5 percent of the national labor force. By 2003, the female proportion was about 46.9 percent in Michigan, and about 46.0 percent nationally.[8]

Since the 1970s, the wage gap between men and women has fallen substantially. As shown in George Johnson's chapter in *Michigan at the Millennium,* the average 40-year-old female worker with a high-school diploma earned about 57.4 percent as much as her male counterpart in 1973. By 2000, this ratio had risen to about 71 percent. Women with college degrees showed similar improvements relative to men with college degrees.[9] As we shall see later in this chapter, the educational attainments of women are increasing much more rapidly than those of men. Also, there is some evidence that the amount of labor-market discrimination against women has decreased. Thus, there are good reasons to believe that the trend toward a smaller gender-earnings gap will continue.

Minorities in the Michigan Labor Force

In 1910, about 99 percent of Michigan's people were non-Hispanic whites, compared with about 89 percent of the population of the United States as a whole. Over the last century, however, both Michigan and the United States have experienced a major increase in racial and ethnic diversity. By 2000, more than 14 percent of Michigan's people were black. This was a slightly higher percentage than in the rest of the country. By 2000, about 3.3 percent of Michigan residents were Hispanic. This is a substantial increase, since Hispanics were virtually nonexistent in Michigan before 1930. However, the Hispanic proportion of the population is still much smaller in Michigan than in the United States as a whole.

As their shares of the population have grown, blacks and Hispanics have also accounted for larger portions of the labor force. However, unemployment rates tend to be higher among minorities than among non-Hispanic whites. Thus, the minority percentage of *workers* is slightly smaller than the minority percentage of the *population*.[10]

Unions in the Michigan Labor Force

Union membership grew rapidly after the passage of the National Labor Relations Act in 1935. American labor unions reached their peak in the 1950s, when about one of every three U.S. workers was a member of a union. Since then, the number of union members has changed very little, while the labor force has grown tremendously. As a result, union members have accounted for a shrinking percentage of the work force. By 2004, only 12.5 percent of U.S. workers were members of labor unions. Throughout this period, the unionized percentage of the Michigan work force has also been falling, although unions have consistently represented a larger fraction of the labor force in Michigan than in most of the rest of the country. In 2004, 21.6 percent of the workers in Michigan were union members. This was the third-highest percentage among the 50 states.[11]

Beneath the surface of these overall rates of unionization, there are substantial differences in the degree of unionization in different sectors of the economy. In particular, public-sector employees are much more heavily unionized than those who work for private employers. Michigan's unionization rates are higher than the national average, both in the public sector and in the private sector: In 2004, 15.9 percent of private-sector workers in Michigan were members of unions, versus 7.9 percent of private-sector workers for the United States as a whole. At the same time, 55.9 percent of public-sector workers in Michigan were union members, while 36.5 percent of public-sector workers in the entire United States were in unions.

Labor unions are complex organizations, and they serve social and political functions, as well as economic ones. Thus, any brief discussion is bound to be incomplete. However, it is clear that unions typically desire to increase the wages and benefits of their workers. There is ample evidence that unions have succeeded in raising their workers' wages and benefits to higher levels than those that would have occurred in a competitive labor market. In *Michigan at the Millennium,* George Johnson of the University of Michigan presents evidence that the wage premium for union membership is around 10 percent for workers with less than a college education. However, once a union has succeeded in pushing the *wages and benefits* above their equilibrium levels, the union typically has much greater difficulty in maintaining *employment.*[12] This has been especially important in the automobile industry in Michigan. In chapter 1, we saw that auto-industry workers in Michigan (who are heavily unionized) earn substantially more than auto-industry workers in the rest of the United States (who are less likely to be in unions). This is part of the reason that auto-industry employment has fared worse in Michigan than in some other parts of the country.

This is *not* to say that all of the industry's woes are the result of unionized workers. Auto-industry management has been less than stellar.[13] But if the problems of the American auto industry are to be solved, union workers will have to be a part of the solution. The cost structure of the Big Three automakers simply cannot be sustained under current market conditions. In October 2005, General Motors reached agreement with the United Auto Workers to reduce pay increases and health-care benefits for workers and retirees. In March 2006, the company announced a program of "accelerated attrition," offering up-front cash to workers who would forego benefits later on. My assessment is that, even though each of these is a very substantial step, the painful adjustments are not yet at an end.

According to calculations by George Fulton and Donald Grimes, the average wage for American workers in autos and light trucks and in motor-vehicle parts outside Michigan was more than $52,000 per year in 2004. The average wage for such workers in Michigan was more than $70,000 per year. Both of these figures are well above the average level of wage earnings for full-time, year-round workers in the United States, which were about $37,000 in 2004. The differences would be even greater if we were to include fringe benefits, which are especially generous for unionized workers in the automobile industry. Thus, the unionized workers in the automobile industry are very well paid in comparison with nonunion workers in the auto industry, and in comparison with workers in other industries. The *sustainable* level of wages and benefits at the auto companies is very good.

The best outcomes will only occur if there is constructive cooperation between labor and management. If workers are to be asked to give up some of their pay and benefits, management must be seen as sharing in the pain. The announcement, in February 2006, of pay reductions for top General Motors executives was a welcome step.[14]

In the long run, the greatest benefits for Michigan's workers will come not from union negotiations, but from education and training. We now turn our attention to educational attainment and education policy.

Educational Attainment in Michigan

Educational attainment is the single most important factor in determining success in the labor market. In this section, we present some measures of educational attainment for Michigan, in addition to comparisons with other states.

Completion of High School and College

Table 2.2 shows the percentage of the population aged 25 and over with at least a high-school education, for the 50 states and the District of Columbia, in 2004.[15] This table shows that nearly 88 percent of Michigan adults have a

TABLE 2.2 Percent of Population Aged Twenty-Five and Older with At Least a High School Education, for States in the United States, 2004

RANK	STATE	PERCENT WITH AT LEAST A H.S. EDUCATION	RANK	STATE	PERCENT WITH AT LEAST A H.S. EDUCATION
1	Minnesota	92.3	27	Maine	87.1
2	Montana	91.9	28	Massachusetts	86.9
3	Wyoming	91.9	29	Illinois	86.8
4	Nebraska	91.3	30	Delaware	86.5
5	Utah	91.0	31	Pennsylvania	86.5
6	New Hampshire	90.8	32	District of Columbia	86.4
7	Vermont	90.8	33	Nevada	86.3
8	Alaska	90.2	34	Florida	85.9
9	Iowa	89.8	35	New York	85.4
10	Washington	89.7	36	Georgia	85.2
11	Kansas	89.6	37	Oklahoma	85.2
12	North Dakota	89.5	38	Arizona	84.4
13	Connecticut	88.8	39	South Carolina	83.6
14	Wisconsin	88.8	40	Mississippi	83.0
15	Virginia	88.4	41	New Mexico	82.9
16	Colorado	88.3	42	Tennessee	82.9
17	Ohio	88.1	43	Alabama	82.4
18	Hawaii	88.0	44	Kentucky	81.8
19	Idaho	87.9	45	California	81.3
20	**Michigan**	**87.9**	46	Rhode Island	81.1
21	Missouri	87.9	47	North Carolina	80.9
22	New Jersey	87.6	48	West Virginia	80.9
23	South Dakota	87.5	49	Arkansas	79.2
24	Maryland	87.4	50	Louisiana	78.7
25	Oregon	87.4	51	Texas	78.3
26	Indiana	87.2		**United States Average**	**85.2**

Source: "Educational Attainment in the United States: 2004", table 13, at http://www.census.gov/population/www/socdemo/education/cps2004.html.

high-school education or more. Michigan's percentage was above the national average of 85.2 percent, and Michigan ranked 20th among the 50 states.

Many of the states with the lowest levels of high-school attainment have large numbers of Hispanic immigrants, who tend to have relatively little education. One reason that Michigan ranks as highly as it does in this category is that Michigan has relatively few Hispanic immigrants. Nevertheless, when it comes to educational achievement for racial and ethnic minorities, Michigan has many of the same problems that are faced by the rest of the country. Some high schools in Michigan have graduation rates close to 100 percent, but the Detroit public schools, with a student body that is overwhelmingly black, have a graduation rate of only 61 percent.[16] Some individual high schools in Detroit have graduation rates well below 50 percent.

Table 2.3 is similar to table 2.2, except that table 2.3 shows the percentage with at least a bachelor's degree. Michigan's position among the states is much lower in terms of college education than high-school education. Among Michigan residents who are at least 25 years old, only 24.4 percent have a college degree. This is below the national average of 27.7 percent, and it puts Michigan in 37th place (or 36th if we exclude the District of Columbia).

As can be seen in figure 2.3, this poor standing in terms of college attainment is not a recent development. For decades, Michigan has consistently had a smaller percentage of college graduates than the national average.[17] On the bright side, the percentage of people with a college education has been increasing in Michigan. However, Michigan has been more than three percentage points below the national average for most of the last quarter of a century. Thus, we find ourselves perpetually behind the curve in terms of the post-high-school educational attainment of our population.

Educational Achievement

The completion rates in the previous section are important, but they do not tell the entire story. Ultimately, an individual's *level of skill* is at least as important as whether she or he has a diploma or other credential.

Of course, "skill" has many dimensions, so that any simple measure of skill is bound to be imperfect. However, one measure of skill that has some merit is the National Assessment of Educational Progress (NAEP), available at *http://nces.ed.gov/nationsreportcard/*. The NAEP allows us to make comparisons

TABLE 2.3 Percent of Population Aged Twenty-Five and Older with At Least a Bachelor's Degree, for States in the United States, 2004

RANK	STATE	PERCENT WITH AT LEAST A BACHELOR'S	RANK	STATE	PERCENT WITH AT LEAST A BACHELOR'S
1	District of Columbia	45.7	27	Montana	25.5
2	Massachusetts	36.7	28	South Dakota	25.5
3	Colorado	35.5	29	Pennsylvania	25.3
4	New Hampshire	35.4	30	North Dakota	25.2
5	Maryland	35.2	31	New Mexico	25.1
6	New Jersey	34.6	32	South Carolina	24.9
7	Connecticut	34.5	33	Nebraska	24.8
8	Vermont	34.2	34	Ohio	24.6
9	Virginia	33.1	35	Nevada	24.5
10	Minnesota	32.5	36	Texas	24.5
11	California	31.7	**37**	**Michigan**	**24.4**
12	Utah	30.8	38	Iowa	24.3
13	New York	30.6	39	Tennessee	24.3
14	Kansas	30.0	40	Maine	24.2
15	Washington	29.9	41	Idaho	23.8
16	Missouri	28.1	42	North Carolina	23.4
17	Arizona	28.0	43	Oklahoma	22.9
18	Georgia	27.6	44	Wyoming	22.5
19	Illinois	27.4	45	Louisiana	22.4
20	Rhode Island	27.2	46	Alabama	22.3
21	Delaware	26.9	47	Indiana	21.1
22	Hawaii	26.6	48	Kentucky	21.0
23	Florida	26.0	49	Mississippi	20.1
24	Oregon	25.9	50	Arkansas	18.8
25	Wisconsin	25.6	51	West Virginia	15.3
26	Alaska	25.5		**United States Average**	**27.7**

Source: "Educational Attainment in the United States: 2004", table 13, http://www.census.gov/population/www/socdemo/education/cps2004.html.

FIGURE 2.3 Percentage of Population Aged 25 and Over with a Bachelor's Degree, for Michigan and the United States, 1977–2004

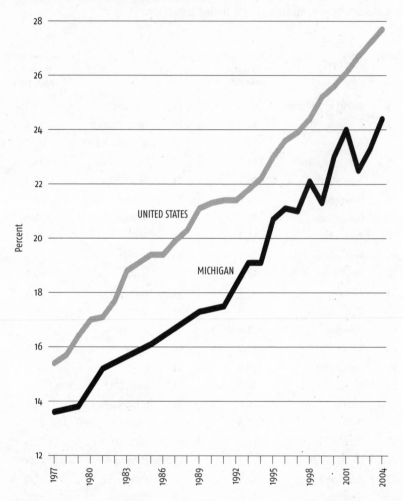

among the states in terms of student achievement on tests in reading, mathematics, and other subjects.

Table 2.4 shows the percentage of students who achieve a "basic" level of achievement on math and reading tests in the fourth and eighth grades. On the basis of these data, the only reasonable conclusion is that Michigan is doing a mediocre job of preparing its children for the future.

TABLE 2.4 Percent of Students Achieving a "Basic" Level of Achievement, as Reported in the National Assessment of Educational Progress, 2005

FOURTH GRADE READING	% AT BASIC LEVEL
U.S. Average	62
Highest State (Massachusetts)	78
Michigan	**63**
Lowest State (Mississippi)	48
District of Columbia	33

Michigan ranks 31st among the 50 states (tied with Arkansas)

FOURTH GRADE MATHEMATICS	% AT BASIC LEVEL
U.S. Average	79
Highest State (Massachusetts)	91
Michigan	**79**
Lowest State (New Mexico)	65
District of Columbia	45

Michigan ranks 31st among the 50 states (tied with Maryland, Missouri, and Oklahoma)

EIGHTH GRADE READING	% AT BASIC LEVEL
U.S. Average	71
Highest State (Massachusetts)	83
Michigan	**73**
Lowest State (Hawaii)	58
District of Columbia	45

Michigan ranks 28th among the 50 states (tied with Indiana and Utah)

EIGHTH GRADE MATHEMATICS	% AT BASIC LEVEL
U.S. Average	68
Highest State (North Dakota)	81
Michigan	**68**
Lowest State (Mississippi)	52
District of Columbia	31

Michigan ranks 31st among the 50 states (tied with Illinois and Missouri)

Michigan's children are very close to the national average in each of the categories shown in table 2.4. If the national average were impressive, then we could celebrate the fact that Michigan is close to the national average. But the national average is not at all impressive. Neither Michigan nor the United States as a whole is anywhere near where it needs to be. In each of the four categories, at least 21 percent of Michigan children are not even achieving at a "basic" level.

The percentages of students achieving at the "proficient" level are much lower than the percentages achieving at the "basic" level. Only 28 percent of Michigan eighth graders were deemed "proficient" in reading, and only 30 percent in mathematics. To put it more bluntly, more than two out of every three Michigan eighth graders are *not* proficient. Each of these figures is close to the national average, but once again the national average is pathetic. If we were to prepare adequately for the future, virtually all students would achieve "basic" competency, and a strong majority would be "proficient."

Table 2.4 shows that the District of Columbia does less well than any of the 50 states in all four of these categories of educational achievement. It is also true that minorities make up a higher percentage of the school population in D.C. than in any of the 50 states. This is no coincidence. In many cases, the states with the lowest percentages achieving the "basic" or "proficient" level are states with relatively large minority populations. America continues to do a poor job of achieving strong educational outcomes for minority children. This is true in Michigan, just as in the rest of the country. Whereas 68 percent of all Michigan eighth graders achieved the "basic" level in math, only 34 percent of black Michigan eighth graders achieved at that level. Some 30 percent of all Michigan eighth graders achieved the "proficient" level in math, but only 6 percent of black Michigan eighth graders did so.

One way to describe the problem is that many of Michigan's young people reach the age of 18 with only a sixth-grade or eighth-grade or tenth-grade education (even though they may have a diploma from a Michigan high school). This is an unconscionable waste of human resources, and it is also a waste of financial resources. At today's level of spending, Michigan taxpayers spend about $100,000 on every student who goes from kindergarten through 12th grade in Michigan public schools. To say the least, it is disappointing for us to spend $100,000 to produce students who do not know how to use fractions, or how to write a paragraph that is clear and grammatically correct. Anyone who spends $100,000 on a house has a right to expect the plumbing and wiring to be in order. And if we spend $100,000 on a child, we have a right to expect the child to have a 12th-grade education.[18]

Later in this chapter, I will offer some thoughts on how to improve educational outcomes for Michigan's children.

Effects of Education on the Level and Distribution of Income

We have seen that Michigan's population is above the U.S. average in attainment of a high-school education, but below the U.S. average in attainment of a college degree. What effects do these educational differences have on incomes? The answer is that, in today's economy, a high level of college attainment is *far* more important for the incomes of a state's people than a high level of high-school attainment.

In chapter 1, we saw the ranking of the 50 states according to per capita personal income. The four states with the highest income levels were Connecticut, Massachusetts, New Jersey, and Maryland. All four of these states are in the top six for college attainment, while they rank quite a bit lower in terms of high-school attainment. This suggests that college education may have the greater influence on income levels. We can go beyond this kind of anecdotal evidence by using the statistical technique of regression analysis. If we analyze per capita personal income for the 50 states and the District of Columbia, on the basis of the educational attainment rates shown in tables 2.2 and 2.3, we find that a higher rate of high-school graduation has essentially no effect on a state's level of personal income (holding constant the level of college attainment). On the other hand, all else equal, an increase of one percentage point in a state's rate of college attainment would lead to an increase of more than $800 of annual income per person. This suggests that if Michigan were at the national average in terms of college attainment, its per capita personal income would be above the national average, rather than below it.

Table 2.5 shows the extent to which labor-market earnings increased with education for the United States as a whole in 2004.[19] The data in table 2.5 are for men, aged 45–54, who worked full-time for the entire year. However, a similar pattern would emerge if we were to look at the numbers for women, or for other age groups. On average, the men in this age group with only a

TABLE 2.5 Average Earnings in 2004, by Level of Education, for Men Ages 45–54 Who Worked Full-Time, Year-Round

LEVEL OF EDUCATION	AVERAGE EARNINGS FROM EMPLOYMENT
Less Than 9th Grade	$ 25,098
Some High School (No Diploma)	33,907
High-School Graduate	44,123
Some College (No Degree)	53,813
Bachelor's Degree	80,301
Master's Degree	103,083
Professional Degree	164,551

Source: United States Bureau of the Census, http://pubdb3.census.gov/macro/032005/perinc/new03_000.htm.

grade-school education earned a little more than $25,000 in 2004. Men with a bachelor's degree earned about $80,000, and those with a professional degree earned about $165,000.

In addition to having higher earnings, people with more education are more likely to be employed. In October 2005, the unemployment rate was 2.3 percent for workers with a bachelor's degree or higher, 3.8 percent for those with some college or an associate's degree, 4.8 percent for those with a high-school diploma but no college, and 7.1 percent for those with less than a high-school diploma.[20]

These facts suggest that gains can be made by increasing education *throughout the entire spectrum of educational attainments.* Michigan's economy will be stronger if we can increase the percentage of the population with a bachelor's degree. This is especially true now, because the payoff for a bachelor's degree is substantially larger than it was a few decades ago. However, bachelor's degrees are not the only game in town. Michigan's economy will also be strengthened by increasing the percentage finishing high school, and by getting more of the high-school graduates to move on to either a community college or a four-year college, and by getting more of those with a bachelor's degree to pursue education beyond college. Moreover, at every step along the way, it is essential to make sure that students are really developing their skills, and not merely getting a credential.

The Beneficial Spillovers of Education

We have seen that an individual is more likely to be employed, and is likely to earn a great deal more, if he or she has more education. However, an increase in the education level of the labor force can also lead to important benefits, even for those who remain with lower levels of education.

This may seem surprising. How can an individual with less education be helped when *someone else* gets more education? For one thing, an increase in a community's educational level can improve the overall productivity of the local economy. Some recent evidence along these lines is presented in a paper by Timothy Bartik of Kalamazoo's Upjohn Institute for Employment Research.[21]

There is also a second reason why increased education has positive spillover effects for those with less education. This has to do with the interaction of supply and demand in labor markets. When there is an increase in the number of college-educated workers, more people will be competing for the top jobs, and fewer will be competing for the jobs at the bottom of the ladder. This will lead to an increase in the wages of workers with less education compared to those with more education. (Workers with more education will still be earning more than those with less education, but the gap will be smaller than it would be if there were no spillovers.)

A dramatic example of this occurred in the United States in the early part of the twentieth century. In 1910, only about 10 percent of young Americans were getting a high-school diploma. But the state legislatures passed laws requiring school districts to provide for a high-school education. If a district did not have a high school of its own, it had to pay to send its children to the nearest high school. (This was greatly facilitated by the growing availability of school buses.) By 1940, about 60 percent were finishing high school. By 1960, that number had increased to well over 80 percent.

This was a revolutionary change. As a result of this expansion of educational opportunity, there was a huge increase in the number of workers who could compete for the better jobs. (Nowadays, a highly skilled worker is usually one with a college degree. But 75 years ago, a high-school diploma was the mark of a highly skilled worker.) At the same time, fewer workers were competing for jobs as laborers, and the wages of laborers rose rapidly. In the first half of the twentieth century, the distribution of income in the United States became dramatically more equal.[22]

Thus, education does more than make the economy more productive. It also leads to greater equality. Of course, educational opportunity has continued to expand in the last 30 years, and yet the distribution of income has become more unequal. This is because the *demand* for highly skilled labor has increased even more rapidly than the *supply* of highly skilled labor. If educational attainment had not continued to expand during the last 30 years, the widening of the income gap between workers with high skills and those with low skills would have been even more severe than it has been. All else equal, however, when more workers become highly skilled, some benefits accrue even to those who do *not* acquire more skill.

The Critical Importance of Higher Education

In the last few years, a number of important studies have looked at higher-education issues. One of these is the report of the Lieutenant Governor's Commission on Higher Education and Economic Growth (known as the "Cherry Commission" after Lt. Governor John D. Cherry Jr.). This report, published in December 2004, is available from *http://www.cherrycommission.org.*

James Duderstadt, president emeritus of the University of Michigan, has been deeply involved in assessing and publicizing the role of higher education. Duderstadt is project director of the Millennium Project, which produced "A Roadmap to Michigan's Future: Meeting the Challenge of a Global Knowledge-Driven Economy" in September 2005. (The Millennium Project does not have any official connection with *Michigan at the Millennium.*) This report is available at http://milproj.ummu.umich.edu/publications/roadmap/.

Finally, the Federal Reserve Bank of Chicago held a conference on "Higher Education at a Crossroad" in November 2005.[23] Papers presented at the conference are available from *http://www.chicagofed.org/news_and_conferences/conferences_and_events/2005_future_of_higher_education_agenda.cfm.*

These three sources contain an enormous wealth of information and analysis, along with articulate commentary. It is far beyond the scope of this short book to summarize these sources adequately. However, I would like to emphasize a few points:

- First of all, as is clear from some of the data presented earlier in this chapter, an individual's *earnings in the labor market* are greater when he or she has more education. This occurs at all levels of education, but the most important jumps in earnings occur for people who go beyond high school. It should be noted that the benefits of higher education do not merely accrue to those who are in school in their late teens and early twenties. In today's economic environment, learning is increasingly a lifelong enterprise, and increasing numbers are returning to college after many years away from school.
- Second, research universities perform a crucial function for society through the development of *basic science and technology.* So many aspects of the high-tech economy, from digital electronics to gene therapies to advanced cancer treatments to logistical management procedures, were built on a foundation of basic research carried out at universities.
- Third, research universities provide an ideal environment for developing *applied science and technology.* Basic research is an essential underpinning for the new technologies that are transforming our lives. However, it is also essential to build on the basic research, so that new products and techniques can be developed and brought to the global market. Michigan's research universities are devoting increased resources to programs for technology transfer.

Michigan is fortunate to have a multi-tiered group of publicly supported institutions of higher learning. The first tier includes the community colleges. These colleges provide a host of opportunities, including hands-on training for the skilled technical jobs that are increasingly important in today's economy. The community colleges also provide many students with a springboard to further education. The second tier of Michigan's higher-education system has 12 regional universities, such as Eastern Michigan University, Grand Valley State University, and Northern Michigan University.

The third tier of the system consists of three research universities: the University of Michigan, Michigan State University, and Wayne State University. The research universities provide educational opportunities for large numbers of students. However, the research universities have a unique role that goes beyond instruction. These universities also provide research capabilities that can have a profound economic impact. For one thing, the research universities bring hundreds of millions of dollars of federal research funds into the state every year. Moreover, many of the laboratory discoveries have commercial applications. Also, the research universities are very actively engaged with the rest of Michigan in terms of economic, social, and cultural-outreach programs. One can get a sense of the breadth and depth of these connections by going to the website of University Outreach and Engagement at Michigan State University, at *http://outreach.msu.edu.*

Even though the research universities are deeply engaged with the state, many of Michigan's people are not very familiar with these contributions. I have had many conversations with Michigan residents who reveal that they have only a very limited idea of the range of work done at the research universities. This brief book is not the place for a comprehensive catalog of all of the activities of the research universities. But I hope I have made clear that the scope of those activities is vast.

Zones of Innovation

The "Silicon Valley" is a narrow strip of land along the southern and western shores of San Francisco Bay. It is home to Hewlett-Packard, Intel, Oracle, and many other dynamic, innovative companies. The Silicon Valley is at the cutting edge of technology, not only for the United States, but for the entire world.

Why is the Silicon Valley located where it is? Why is it not in Idaho, or Nebraska, or Alabama? One important reason is the close proximity of Stanford University and the University of California at Berkeley. Across the country, when we find regions at the cutting edge in technology and innovation, universities are always nearby.

Could something like the Silicon Valley happen in Michigan? To a certain extent, it is already happening. As discussed in the *Michigan at the Millennium* chapter by Abel Feinstein, George Fulton, and Donald Grimes, Michigan has become a worldwide leader in automotive high technology. More importantly, Michigan has tremendous potential to become a much greater center of innovation. If this is to occur, Michigan's universities are certain to play a crucial role.

When we take the University of Michigan, Michigan State University, and Wayne State University, we have three institutions of a caliber that is absent in most of the 50 states. These institutions can provide a platform for future economic growth in Michigan. Unfortunately, policy makers in Michigan have slashed higher-education budgets in recent years. But the precious resource of our colleges and universities has not been squandered, at least not yet. The colleges and universities still provide tremendous benefits to the Michigan economy, and they have even greater potential.

The Brain Drain

If Michigan is to achieve its economic potential, it is crucial to *train* educated workers, but it is also necessary to *retain* them. When highly educated workers migrate to other regions of the country, Michigan loses out. In fact, outmigration of young people is a serious problem for Michigan. In his *Michigan at the Millennium* chapter on population, Kenneth Darga points out that Michigan suffered a net loss in the 1990s of nearly 60,000 residents aged 20 to 31.

This outward migration is partly due to military service: young Michigan residents who enter the armed forces will almost always leave the state for military bases in the south and west. However, much of the out-migration has nothing to do with military service. In order to retain talented young people, Michigan has to create and maintain the kind of atmosphere that will make these people want to stay here. In the best-selling book *The Rise of the Creative Class* (New York: Perseus Books, 2002), Richard Florida emphasizes the increasingly important economic role played by creative people in science and engineering, design, education, arts, and entertainment. These people are disproportionately located in metropolitan areas, but not just in any metropolitan areas. Mr. Florida stresses the "3 T's" of economic development—technology, talent, and tolerance. Thus, although Mr. Florida does not explicitly use the phrase "Cool Cities," he is basically talking about the same thing.

The Rise of the Creative Class lists rankings of cities along various dimensions associated with creativity. The highest overall scores go to San Francisco, Austin, Boston, San Diego, and Seattle, all of which are fairly large. However, Mr. Florida also mentions a number of smaller cities that score well in some of these dimensions. These include Ann Arbor and East Lansing, as well as Bloomington, Indiana; Champaign-Urbana, Illinois; Iowa City,

Iowa; Madison, Wisconsin; and State College, Pennsylvania. Clearly, university communities have some of the greatest potential for harnessing the forces of economic innovation.

The Relative Decline in College Attainment for Men

Before closing this discussion of the importance of colleges and universities, I want to mention one issue that has received relatively little attention. The issue is illustrated in figure 2.4, which shows that men have accounted for a steadily decreasing percentage of newly awarded bachelor's degrees in the United States in recent decades. In 1960–61, about 61.5 percent of the newly conferred bachelor's degrees went to men. By 2001–02, that percentage had decreased to about 42.6 percent.[24]

Figure 2.4 is the result of both good news and bad news. The good news is that American women have increased their educational attainment dramatically. About 140,000 women got a bachelor's degree in 1961. This number increased steadily, to about 420,000 in 1976, and about 775,000 in 2003. The bad news is that American men have not advanced nearly as much. The number of bachelor's degrees awarded to American men was almost exactly the same in 1999 as it had been in 1973. A similar trend has occurred in the awards of associate degrees, about 60 percent of which now go to women. Men still receive slightly more than half of the doctorate degrees, but that does not change the overall picture. While women have achieved exceptional increases in their educational attainment, men have made relatively little progress.

Financing Education in Michigan

The case has been made for the importance of education at all levels, including elementary, secondary, and post-secondary education. Now we turn to the question of how to pay for it.

Educational Productivity

If we can improve productivity in the educational system, it may be possible to achieve better educational outcomes at very low cost. Unfortunately, there are limits to our ability to improve productivity in education.

FIGURE 2.4 Bachelor's Degrees Received by Men as Percent of Total Bachelor's Degrees, in the United States, 1961–2003

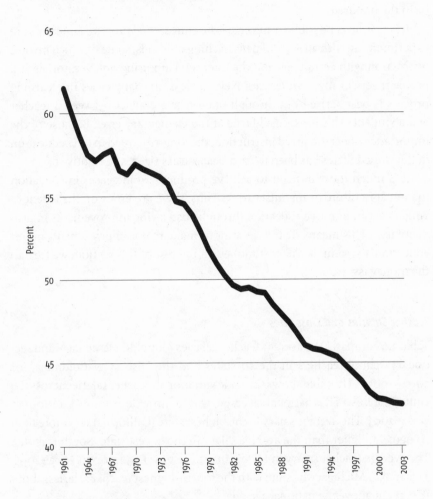

In chapter 1 of this book, we discussed the huge productivity improvements in agriculture and manufacturing. The average farm worker in Michigan today can produce far more food than the average farm worker of decades ago. The average factory worker of today can produce far more manufactured goods than the average factory worker of decades ago. But today's average classroom teacher does not (and should not) teach several times as many children as the average classroom teacher of a few decades back. If educational productivity had increased at the same rate as productivity in manufacturing and agriculture, elementary and secondary class sizes would be in the hundreds.

It is *sometimes* possible to automate the educational process. Educators are experimenting with all sorts of new teaching methods, some of which involve instruction with computers and the Internet. I am using online tutorials and problem sets in my own classes. Nevertheless, in many cases the learning process is best carried out through one-on-one contact between a teacher and a student. This is especially true at the elementary level. Because of the importance of personalized instruction, the long-run trend in K–12 education in the United States has been toward *smaller* class sizes, and rightly so.

It is much more difficult to achieve productivity increases in education than in agriculture or manufacturing. Thus, there are limits on the extent to which we can improve education through cost-saving improvements in productivity.[25] This means that if we want to make major improvements in our educational system, it will cost money. In the rest of this section, we turn to the money issues.

Teacher Salaries and Class Sizes

Table 2.6 compares the average teacher salaries for public elementary and secondary school teachers in the 50 states and the District of Columbia, for 2002–2003.[26] The table shows the wide variation in teacher salaries across the United States. The national average was a little less than $46,000 in 2002–2003. The average salary in the highest state (California) was more than 70 percent higher than the average salary in the lowest state (South Dakota). The average teacher salary in Michigan was just over $54,000 in 2002–2003. This makes Michigan the state with the fourth-highest teacher salaries, about 18 percent above the national average.

In response to the relatively high teacher salaries, it would make sense for school districts in Michigan to try to exert some control over expenditures by having larger class sizes. In fact, in the 1999–2000 school year, elementary-school class sizes in Michigan were about 4 percent larger than the national average. In that same year, secondary-school class sizes in Michigan were about 7 percent above the national average.[27] As I see it, a strong case can be

TABLE 2.6 Average Teacher Salaries in the Fifty States, 2002–2003

RANK	STATE	AVERAGE TEACHER SALARIES	RANK	STATE	AVERAGE TEACHER SALARIES
1	California	$56,283	27	Colorado	41,275
2	Connecticut	54,362	28	Arizona	40,894
3	New Jersey	54,166	29	New Hampshire	40,519
4	**Michigan**	**54,071**	30	Idaho	40,148
5	New York	52,600	31	Texas	40,001
6	Massachusetts	52,043	32	Tennessee	39,677
7	Pennsylvania	51,800	33	Florida	39,465
8	Illinois	51,289	34	Kentucky	38,981
9	Rhode Island	51,076	35	Iowa	38,921
10	Delaware	50,772	36	Missouri	38,826
11	District of Columbia	50,763	37	West Virginia	38,508
12	Alaska	49,685	38	Utah	38,413
13	Maryland	49,677	39	Alabama	38,246
14	Oregon	47,600	40	Kansas	38,123
15	Georgia	45,533	41	Maine	38,121
16	Ohio	45,452	42	Nebraska	37,896
17	Indiana	45,097	43	Wyoming	37,876
18	Washington	44,949	44	Arkansas	37,753
19	Hawaii	44,464	45	Louisiana	36,878
20	Virginia	43,152	46	New Mexico	36,687
21	North Carolina	43,076	47	Montana	35,754
22	Wisconsin	42,871	48	Oklahoma	34,854
23	Minnesota	42,833	49	Mississippi	34,555
24	Nevada	41,795	50	North Dakota	33,210
25	Vermont	41,603	51	South Dakota	32,416
26	South Carolina	41,279		**United States Average**	**$45,822**

Source: Digest of Education Statistics, 2004, table 78, http://nces.ed.gov/programs/digest/d04/tables/dt04_078.asp.

made for keeping class sizes small. This will require some combination of additional financial resources for the schools, and/or moderation in teacher pay.

Proposal A and the Financing of K–12 Education

In 1994, Michigan voters approved Proposal A, which brought about dramatic changes in the financing of elementary and secondary education. Proposal A involved major changes in the sales tax and the cigarette tax, but its greatest effects on Michigan's tax system were associated with the property tax. Thus, readers who want to know more about the details of Proposal A can consult the chapter on property taxes in *Michigan at the Millennium* by Naomi Feldman and Paul Courant of the University of Michigan, and Douglas Drake of Wayne State University. Proposal A also led to large changes in per-pupil expenditures in school districts throughout the state. Readers may also be interested in the *Michigan at the Millennium* chapter on K–12 education by Julie Cullen of the University of Michigan and Susanna Loeb of Stanford University.

Prior to Proposal A, local public schools in Michigan were financed mainly by local property taxes. Under this system, there were huge disparities between the funding levels in rich school districts and poor school districts. However, as a result of Proposal A, *local* property taxes were reduced dramatically, while several *state* taxes were increased. Consequently, much of the power to make decisions about the public schools was shifted from the local level to the state level. After Proposal A, a large part of the decision-making process for school finance was moved to the Lansing offices of the legislature and the governor.

Since the passage of Proposal A, the state government has provided a system of per-pupil "foundation allowances" for operating expenses in the public schools. The minimum foundation allowance, which goes to low-revenue school districts, has increased much more rapidly than the allowances for higher-revenue districts. After adjusting for inflation, the per-pupil funding levels in the poorest school districts have increased by about one-fourth, while the funding levels in many affluent districts have increased at a much slower pace, and the funding for some of the richest districts has actually decreased. Thus, the difference between the funding levels in the rich districts and the poor districts has fallen dramatically. In 1994, the per-pupil operating revenues in the ten highest-revenue districts were about 2.8 times as large as those in the ten lowest-revenue districts. By 2003, the foundation allowances for the top ten districts were still larger than the allowances for the bottom ten districts, but only by a factor of 1.7.[28]

Before Proposal A, it was difficult for Michigan's poorest school districts to provide even minimally acceptable levels of instruction. Of course, the increases in funding for the poorest districts do not *guarantee* that the children in those districts will be educated adequately, but at least the additional funding improves the chances that these children will get a good education. In fact, the evidence suggests that the increased funding for schools did improve educational outcomes. Leslie Papke of Michigan State University has studied the effects of spending on pass rates for the fourth-grade math test. She uses data for individual schools in Michigan for the years before and after the passage of Proposal A. Papke finds that an increase in real, inflation-adjusted spending leads to an increase in the test pass rate. Importantly, the increases were larger for the schools that were performing poorly before Proposal A.[29]

I have emphasized the fact that the distribution of income has become much more unequal over the last 30 years. The trend toward greater inequality has been exacerbated by many of the policies undertaken in Michigan. However, there is one major exception to this pattern, and that is the move toward more uniform levels of funding across school districts.

Financing Capital Expenditures in Michigan's Public Schools

Proposal A reduced the school-funding disparities between rich districts and poor districts, for *operating expenditures*. However, Proposal A did not apply to *capital expenditures*. As a result, the revenues for school construction, school renovation, and other capital expenditures are still drawn almost exclusively from local sources. Although the poorer school districts are now better able to pay for operating expenditures, they are still at a tremendous disadvantage when it comes to capital spending.

This issue is analyzed in an excellent report issued recently by the Citizens Research Council of Michigan (CRC) and the Educational Policy Center (EPC) at Michigan State University.[30] The report's authors emphasize that there are huge differences in the amount of taxable property in the various school districts in Michigan. In the 29 wealthiest districts, the value of taxable property per student is more than $500,000. In the 75 least-wealthy districts, there is less than $100,000 of taxable property per pupil. The six poorest districts (which include Detroit) have less than $50,000 per student. As a result, many of the poorest districts have aging and inadequate school facilities. (For example, more than half of the schools in Detroit were built before 1930.) This is not because the poor districts have low tax rates. In fact, the property-tax rates in many of the poorest districts are well above the state average. The problem is that these districts simply do not have a tax base that is large enough to pay for adequate school facilities, regardless of their property-tax rates.

Because of Proposal A, individual school districts no longer have the option of raising more tax revenues for operating expenditures (even if the voters in the district would prefer to do so). However, the districts still can commit themselves to higher property taxes in the future by approving bond issues for capital expenditures. Since local districts have lost flexibility regarding operating expenditures, but still retain flexibility in terms of capital expenditures, it is probably not surprising that the volume of capital expenditure has increased dramatically since 1994.

By treating capital expenditures so differently from operating expenditures, Michigan's policies may encourage inefficient use of resources. For example, consider the fact that new school buses are capital expenditures, whereas repairs on old buses are operating expenditures. As a result of this distinction, a school district may have an incentive to buy new school buses before the old buses have completed their useful lives.

In the school districts with high levels of taxable property, it has been possible to build newer and better facilities without raising property-tax rates to prohibitive levels. These new facilities can then be used to attract additional students from poorer districts nearby, under Michigan's program of public schools of choice. This puts the poorer districts in a vicious cycle: Unable to build new facilities, they lose students. When they lose students, they also lose the foundation-grant funds that go with those students. The loss of foundation-grant funds puts even more financial pressure on the poor districts, and the cycle continues.

The authors of the CRC/EPC report calculate the cost of providing every K–12 student in Michigan with an adequate physical infrastructure at school. (Note that these calculations are based on conservative assumptions about the quality of the new facilities that would be built. If the capital expenditures envisioned in the CRC/EPC report were undertaken, the new facilities would be better than the old ones they replace, but they would not be as elaborate as some of the facilities that have been built recently in some affluent districts.) The CRC/EPC report suggests that the value of unmet capital needs in Michigan public schools is about $8.9 billion. About one-fourth of the total need is found in five low-income school districts in central cities: Battle Creek, Detroit, Flint, Muskegon, and Saginaw.

The figure of $8.9 billion of unmet capital needs may sound daunting. However, we should remember that capital expenditures can be financed over a long period of time. The CRC/EPC authors note that if we were to finance these new capital investments over a period of 30 years at 5 percent interest, it would add less than 5 percent to the annual amount that is now spent on public schools in Michigan.

Any successful reform of Michigan's school-finance system must shift some of the financial responsibility for school capital infrastructure from the local districts to the state government. As long as capital projects are exclusively a local responsibility, there is simply no way that the poorest districts can provide adequate facilities for their children. The authors of the CRC/EPC report discuss various proposals for addressing the unmet capital needs in Michigan's public schools. One option would be a system of "district power equalization," under which the state would subsidize the per-pupil yield of each mill of the local property tax in order to bring each district's revenue-raising capacity up to a guaranteed minimum level. Other proposals range from modest changes in the state's School Bond Loan Fund program, to a more drastic proposal under which the state would assume full responsibility for all financing of investments in public-school infrastructure.

Regardless of which plan is adopted, *something* needs to be done. The current policy says, in effect, that some Michigan children do not deserve to be educated in decent facilities. And yet Michigan's children cannot reach their full educational potential when they are stuck in dilapidated and antiquated facilities. It is useful to recall that, even though Michigan's economy has not performed very well in recent decades, we are not a poor state. There is no question that we can afford to send all of our children to school in decent facilities. And yet we choose not to.

How Equal Should School Funding Be?

Until the mid-1990s, there were enormous disparities among Michigan school districts, both in per-pupil operating expenditures and in per-pupil capital expenditures. As we have seen, Proposal A reduced the disparities for operating expenditures, but not for capital expenditures. I have praised the move toward greater equality in operating expenditures, and I have proposed that we also move toward greater equality in capital expenditures.

However, I want to make the case *against* equalizing *completely*. It is appropriate to bring every student up to a decent standard, regardless of how wealthy or poor the child's school district might be. But once we provide a solid level of expenditure for every child in the state (for capital needs as well as for operating needs), I have no objection to allowing voters in the affluent school districts to spend more on their own children, if they choose to do so. In fact, it would be dangerous to insist on completely equal per-pupil expenditures throughout the state.

There are two important reasons for avoiding complete equalization. First, the economy of the future will be increasingly dominated by talented and creative people. In order to attract the top talent, Michigan needs to have at least some school districts that are truly excellent. Second, if middle-class and upper-middle-class voters were ever to reach the conclusion that they are completely unable to provide the desired level of educational expenditures for their children, there is a danger that they would withdraw their political support for public education in general. (This may already have occurred to a certain extent.) If very large numbers of affluent parents pull their children out of public schools (either to private schools or to home schooling), it would have devastating effects on the entire system of K–12 education throughout the state. Even if very few affluent children leave the public schools, complete equalization could still lead to a general loss of support for the schools.[31]

For many years, Michigan tilted heavily toward local control of all types of school spending, with only a minor role for state government. Proposal A took Michigan to the other extreme for school operating expenditures, and left very little maneuvering room for the individual school districts. I have made a case here for a more balanced mixture of state control and local control of public-school financing, both for operating expenditures and for capital expenditures. There are vast differences among school districts in the ability to raise revenue, and this suggests that there is an important role for state financing so that even the children in the poorest areas can receive an adequate education. However, if every school district in Michigan is given the financial resources to educate its children adequately, there are good reasons not to prohibit the more affluent districts from spending more on their own students, if that is what their voters decide to do.

Financing Retirement Benefits for Michigan Teachers

Michigan has also made one other important change in the division of school-financing responsibility between the state government and the local school districts. Prior to Proposal A, the state government and the school districts shared in paying for the employer portion of contributions to the Michigan Public School Employees Retirement System (MPSERS). However, after Proposal A was approved, the full responsibility was placed on the shoulders of the local districts. Thus, at the very time when local districts were losing their ability to raise their own revenues, they were given an additional financial responsibility. This has intensified the financial squeeze on school districts.

The percentage of payroll going to contributions for retirement programs has been rising, and it is expected to continue to rise. Through 2008, the system will see increased pension contributions, to offset the large investment losses suffered by pension funds in 2001–2002.[32]

The health-care benefits of retired teachers present a much more serious problem than the pension benefits. The health-care benefits have always been handled on a pay-as-you-go basis. Whereas Michigan teacher pensions are paid from assets accumulated in advance, this is not done for the health-care benefits. Also, health-care costs in the United States have been rising rapidly over a long period, and they are expected to continue to rise at a faster rate than the general rate of inflation. According to calculations by the Citizens Research Council of Michigan, the unfunded accrued liability for health benefits in the MPSERS was nearly $16 *billion* in 2003.[33]

According to that same report, the combined contribution rate for pension and health benefits in MPSERS is projected to rise from about 15 percent of payroll in 2005 to about 32 percent of payroll by 2020. Already, burgeoning pension and health-care costs are forcing many school districts to make painful reductions in their instructional programs. Since 2003, the increases in the foundation grant have been very modest, and the additional funds have not been enough to cover the rising pension and health-care costs. Under the current system, where public schools are not given additional resources to pay for these costs, it appears likely that the pressure on instructional programs will only become more severe over time.

In many of Michigan's school districts, inflation-adjusted funding levels went up substantially during the 1990s. This made it possible to improve instruction. However, if the current policies are not changed, it is possible to imagine a time in the not-too-distant future when all of the progress will have been wiped out by a combination of limited funding, and spiraling pension and health-care costs.

Ultimately, the people of Michigan will have to face up to some very difficult choices. It will be necessary to increase expenditures greatly, or to reduce the promised benefits drastically, or to choose some combination of spending increases and benefit reductions.[34] My hope is that a compromise can be worked out under which some of the responsibility for solving this problem is borne by the taxpaying public, and some is borne by the school employees. If financial support from the state is not increased, and if the teachers and other school employees do not make any concessions, the only alternative is for the schoolchildren to bear the entire burden. In terms of providing for future generations, it is hard to imagine a worse scenario that that.

It is worthwhile to elaborate on the point of the preceding paragraph. If taxes are not raised, then the brunt of the problem will most likely be borne by teachers (in the form of reduced pay and/or reduced benefits), or by schoolchildren (in the form of lower-quality instruction). If teacher benefits are protected completely, then the brunt of the problem will most likely be borne by taxpayers (in the form of higher taxes) or by schoolchildren. In the strongest possible terms, I argue that school budgets should not be balanced on the backs of schoolchildren. If the children are spared, then it may be possible to reduce some other spending programs, but the largest effects will probably be either higher taxes, or lower pay and benefits for teachers. I suggest that the burden should not fall exclusively on taxpayers, nor exclusively on teachers. Yes, there should be some tax increases. (In fact, tax effort in Michigan has fallen substantially in the last few decades. I will return to this issue in chapter 5.) But teachers should not be immune. We have already seen that teacher pay in Michigan is far above the national average. Fringe benefits for teachers are also generous. It is not asking too much for teachers to pay more for their health care, especially at a time when many private-sector workers are doing the same.

When I say that *both* teachers and taxpayers should contribute to the solution, I realize that some people on either side will see my words as heresy. Anti-tax groups insist on further tax cuts, which means the budget must be balanced on the backs of teachers and schoolchildren. Teachers would prefer to see guaranteed funding increases. (Currently, an effort is underway to place a proposal to that effect before the voters.) This would mean that the budget must be balanced exclusively on the backs of taxpayers, or perhaps through cuts to other programs. In my view, neither of these approaches is satisfactory.

Financing Higher Education

I have repeatedly emphasized the crucial importance of higher education. In this light, it makes sense that Michigan should strive to achieve a substantial increase in the annual number of college graduates in the state. For example, the Cherry Commission recommends that the annual number of college graduates should be doubled. This raises the question of how we would pay for the increasing numbers of college students.

The first point to understand is that the state-supported universities in Michigan are already at or near capacity. If we were to double the number of students, it would be necessary to build new classrooms and laboratories, and to hire new faculty members. This will cost money. Second, federal funding for higher education is shrinking. This is a serious mistake on the part of the federal government, but it is doubtful whether Michigan can change the direction of federal policy. Third, the universities are aggressively engaged in private fundraising, and the money raised through those channels can make a big difference. However, if enrollment at Michigan's universities were to increase substantially, it is very unlikely that private endowments could cover all of the additional costs. Thus, if the *people of Michigan* are serious about improving our higher-education outcomes, it will almost certainly be necessary for the *people of Michigan* to provide additional financial resources.

If the state government were to increase its support for higher education, it would be easier for the colleges and universities to accommodate an increase in the number of students. In addition, the colleges and universities themselves can affect the affordability of a college education by adjusting their tuition and financial-aid policies. At many institutions of higher learning, large numbers of students pay less than the full amount of tuition. In effect, many students receive a price discount in the form of financial aid. Under a program of need-based financial aid, students from the most affluent families would pay the full amount of tuition, and students from families of modest means would pay less, on net. (For example, Harvard University recently announced that students from families with income below $60,000 would be exempt from paying tuition.)

A large percentage of students from the most affluent families will go to college in any event. Students from low- and middle-income families are the ones who are making decisions about whether to go to college on the basis of financial considerations.[35] Thus, if we are to increase the number of college graduates, special attention must be focused on students from low- and middle-income families. This means that a policy of higher tuition with more financial aid will reap bigger dividends than a policy of lower tuition with less financial aid. A policy of higher tuition and more financial aid can also be more effective at leveraging federal financial-aid dollars. I am *not* calling for big increases in tuition at the public universities in Michigan. If pushed too far, such a policy could force many students from affluent families to leave the state. The best combination of policies would involve strong financial support from the state, so that tuition can remain at moderate levels, coupled with aggressive financial aid. Regardless of the tuition policies of the colleges and universities, it makes sense to increase the percentage of our financial-aid dollars that are allocated on the basis of need.

Getting Value for Our Education Dollars

Although funding is important, *student effort, student motivation,* and *parent involvement* are also extremely important. It is not easy to increase effort, motivation, and involvement in today's culture, where skipping school is often seen as cool, and studious youngsters are lampooned as nerds. It may be a tall order, but it is one we cannot ignore.

Student effort has many dimensions, but certainly an important dimension is the amount of time spent in school. In the United States, most public schools currently have about 175 or 180 days of instruction per year, with a three-month summer vacation. This schedule may have made sense in the nineteenth century, when most children were expected to spend the summer working in the fields. But it is badly out of step with today's needs. Huge amounts of time are wasted every autumn reviewing the things that were learned the previous spring but forgotten over the summer. The long summer of mental hibernation does more harm to some groups than to others. The economist Alan Krueger suggests that students from families of low socioe-conomic status learn about as much during the school year as those from families of high socioeconomic status, but that the students from low-status families fall further behind during the summer months.[36] If the people of Michigan are serious about preparing their children for the future, they should consider providing the resources to increase the length of the school year, perhaps to 190 or 195 days.[37]

Of course, the number of years of schooling is every bit as important as the number of school days per year. Currently, youngsters in Michigan are re-quired to attend school until age 16. The evidence suggests that compulsory schooling laws are effective in getting some students to stay in school. Fur-thermore, the students who are compelled to stay in school earn higher wages as a result of their extra schooling.[38] Thus, there is a strong argument in favor of increasing the age of compulsory school attendance to 17 or 18.

An increase in the age of compulsory attendance could be one part of a strategy to reduce the number of high-school dropouts, but it should not be the only method. The public schools in Michigan should increase their efforts to identify at-risk students at an early age. Alternative high schools can provide an appropriate environment for students who struggle in regular high schools. (Of course, these programs will only succeed if they are adequately funded.) In the next section, I will discuss some curriculum issues that are also important for the campaign to reduce the number of high-school dropouts.

Just as it is important to keep teenagers in school, it is also important to get young children off to an early start. Increased funding for early-childhood education programs can play an important role in helping children to prepare for school. This can be especially important for children from disadvantaged backgrounds. For a discussion of education policy for preschool children, see Janet Currie, "Early Childhood Education Programs" (*Journal of Economic Per-spectives* 15 2001: 213–38).

Just as there are advantages to early-childhood educational programs, there are also advantages to getting the most out of kindergarten. In terms of preparing children for subsequent grades in school, full-day kindergarten has advantages over half-day kindergarten. Currently, school districts in Michigan receive the full foundation grant for every kindergartner, even though the school districts have the option of offering kindergarten for only half of the day. In other words, when a school district offers full-day kindergarten, it does not receive any more funding than a district with half-day kindergarten, even though the full-day option is obviously more costly. One possible reform would be for the state to require all kindergartners to participate in a full-day program (as long as adequate funding is provided). Another possibility would be to allow districts to offer half-day kindergarten, but to provide a greater foundation allowance for full-day students than for half-day students.

Before I leave the subject of student effort, I would like to mention the issue of repetition (or the lack of it). Most of us get better and better as we do things over and over again. And yet, based on my personal observations, it appears that repetition is out of fashion in the public schools. Repetition is not very fun or exciting, but it is essential. Interestingly, no one ever questions the importance of repetition and drill in sports. *Of course* the football coach practices the sweep play again and again. We all understand that football teams will have a better chance of winning games if the players practice, over and over again. The same determination to improve through practice does not seem to be so widely accepted when it comes to academics.

Curriculum Issues in the Public Schools

I have suggested that children should spend more time in school, but I have said little about what subjects the students should study. In my view, a large fraction of the additional effort should be devoted to mathematics and science. (A friend once said that children ought to take every math course twice. In view of the poor math competency of some of my students, that does not seem like much of an exaggeration.)

However, I want to stress that students should *not* all be shoehorned into a one-size-fits-all curriculum. As this book is being written, high-school graduation requirements in Michigan are being made more stringent. Soon, every child will be required to take four years of English, four years of math, three years of science, three years of social studies, and two years of a foreign language—and to fulfill some other requirements as well. Basically, every child will be required to take a college-preparatory curriculum. In my view, it makes sense to increase graduation requirements, but it also makes sense to maintain some flexibility for those children for whom a college-preparatory curriculum may not be the best.

It may seem ironic that I am expressing skepticism about the new curriculum, since I have spent so much of this chapter emphasizing the benefits of a college education. However, just because Michigan would benefit from a large increase in the size of its college-educated population, it does not follow that every single child must go to college. A more vocationally oriented high-school curriculum may be better for some children.[39] And yet, the new requirements may force cash-strapped school districts to reduce their offerings of courses that would be appropriate for students who are not going to college. This may even encourage some students to drop out of high school: if a college-prep curriculum is forced upon all students, it may be an even greater challenge for those who are not college-bound to stay in high school.

The new law imposes new requirements on the school districts. All else equal, this will intensify the financial squeeze on the districts. Of course, it would be possible for the state government to increase the foundation allowance in order to accommodate the changes. As of this writing, however, it is not clear that this will occur. It is bad policy for the state to pile new requirements on the school districts without providing them with the necessary financial resources. If the State of Michigan is going to require school districts to expand their programs, then the State of Michigan should increase the foundation grant appropriately.

A final problem with the new curriculum requirements is that they may cause some school districts to water down some courses in an effort to help the weaker students to pass. I doubt whether watered-down versions of college-preparatory courses are an improvement, either for weaker students or stronger ones.

I expect this one-size-fits-all curriculum to cause more problems than it solves. In my view, it would have been better to adopt a curriculum that is more rigorous for most students, but which maintains flexibility. I hope Michigan's leaders will revisit the issue. If the new curriculum goes ahead, I hope its effects will be evaluated closely, and that we pay attention to whether it is doing a good job of serving *all* of Michigan's children.

Conclusion

In this chapter, we have looked at Michigan's human resources. We began with a survey of the trends in population and the labor force. The population of Michigan grew very rapidly for most of the twentieth century, but the rate of population growth dropped off sharply after 1970. In the last few decades, the greatest amounts of population growth have occurred in counties on the fringes of the metropolitan areas in the southern Lower Peninsula. The population of the Upper Peninsula has been stagnant for a century, and the populations of some central cities have declined since the 1950s. Detroit's population has fallen by about one million since 1950.

Michigan's population is aging, and the trend toward an older population is expected to accelerate in Michigan, as in the rest of the United States. About one out of every seven Michigan residents is African American, which is a slightly higher proportion than in the United States as a whole. The number of Hispanics in Michigan has grown rapidly in recent decades, but Hispanics still account for less than 4 percent of the Michigan population, which is far less than the proportion for the rest of the United States.

As in the rest of the country, the labor-force participation of Michigan women has increased rapidly. Today, about 47 percent of the workers in Michigan are female. Also, the gender gap in pay has reduced as women have increased their education and their labor-market experience, and labor-market discrimination against women has lessened.

Michigan's labor force has long been more heavily unionized than the labor force of the rest of the United States. However, the percentage of workers who are in unions has decreased over time, both in Michigan and elsewhere. By 2004, 21.6 percent of Michigan workers were union members, compared with 12.5 percent of workers in the United States as a whole. In Michigan, as in the rest of the country, unionization is far more prevalent in the public sector than in the private sector. In 2004, about 56 percent of public-sector workers in Michigan were union members, compared with about 16 percent of private-sector workers.

After the initial sections on population and labor force, the bulk of this chapter has been devoted to educational issues. Although the percentage of adults with a high-school education is higher in Michigan than in the rest of the

United States, the percentage with a college education has lagged persistently behind the national average. This has powerful implications for incomes, since the earnings gap between workers with a college education and those without a college education has been growing for the last 30 years. If the college-educated proportion of the work force in Michigan were as high as in the rest of the country, Michigan's incomes would be above the national average, rather than below it.

There are huge disparities in labor-market earnings among groups with different levels of education. This suggests the benefits of a strategy to increase the educational attainments of Michigan workers, at *all* levels. Essentially, Michigan is underinvested at every level of education, from preschool to Ph.D. The State of Michigan will have a stronger economy if we can:

- Use early-childhood education programs to make sure that every child gets off to a good start in school;
- Increase the amount learned by students in our K–12 schools, regardless of whether they continue their education beyond high school;
- Reduce the number of high-school dropouts;
- Increase the proportion of high-school graduates who go on to college;
- Increase the proportion of college students who complete a degree; and
- Increase the proportion of college graduates who continue their education beyond a bachelor's degree.

These improvements will only occur if the people of Michigan are willing to work for them and pay for them. In other words, they will only happen if we can achieve *changes in our culture,* as well as *changes in our methods of financing education.*

Education and skill play a crucial role in the modern economy. Unfortunately, Michigan has a culture that is not always well suited to these modern realities. In a sense, the Michigan economy of today is a victim of the success of the Michigan economy in years past. In the middle of the twentieth century, it was sensible for many young people to end their education without going to college, because they could get high-paying factory jobs without a college education. "I don't need to study, and I don't need to go to college" is an attitude that lingers in Michigan, even though it has largely outlived its usefulness.

If Michigan's economy is to achieve its potential, the attitudes of the past must be replaced by a new set of attitudes. In other words, in terms of its approach to learning, Michigan needs to develop a new culture. Our young people need to achieve more in school (especially in science and mathematics), but it will be very difficult for them to do so as long as the culture prizes MTV over study, and caricatures the good student as a nerd.

Much of this chapter has been devoted to issues of educational finance. If the culture moves in the right direction, some of the financial issues may take care of themselves. Nevertheless, the financial issues are important in and of themselves. Thus, we end this chapter with a brief summary of ideas regarding the financial side of the educational system.

- It is much more difficult to improve productivity in education than in agriculture or manufacturing. Therefore, we probably will not be able to make the necessary improvements to our educational system without devoting more resources to education.
- Since the passage of Proposal A in 1994, the lowest-spending school districts in Michigan have seen substantial increases in their per-student operating expenditures. A recent study has shown that this has succeeded in improving test scores. This is a major step forward. On the other hand, Proposal A has concentrated the power to make decisions about school operating expenses in the hands of the state government. Some of the wealthier districts would probably choose to increase their expenditures if they were allowed to do so. I have made the case for loosening the restrictions on local school boards in the wealthier districts, as long as adequate funding is provided for the poorer districts.
- As a result of Proposal A, the gap in per-student spending between the highest-spending school districts and the lowest-spending districts has been reduced substantially for *operating expenditures*. However, Proposal A did not apply to *capital expenditures*. Thus, many of the poorest school districts have aging and inadequate facilities. A recent study suggests that it would cost about $8.9 billion to provide every student in Michigan with adequate school facilities. To address this problem, it will be necessary to shift some of the financial responsibility for school capital spending from the local school districts to the state government.
- The unfunded accrued liability for health benefits for retired teachers is estimated at $16 billion. This is another area where it will be necessary to shift some financial responsibility from local school districts to the state government.

• The Lieutenant Governor's Commission on Higher Education and Economic Growth has identified the need for a substantial increase in the number of Michigan residents who receive education beyond high school. It will not be possible to make progress in this direction without spending money. Unfortunately, the State of Michigan has reduced its higher-education spending in recent years.

In terms of the development of human resources, Michigan is at a crossroads. Our educational system and our attitudes toward education are better suited to the economic realities of 50 years ago, or even 100 years ago, than to the realities of today. An extremely important challenge facing Michigan today is to provide adequate funding for education at all levels, and to make sure those funds are well spent.

NOTES

1. These data are from the website of the U.S. Bureau of the Census, at http://www .census.gov/popest/states/tables/NST-EST2005–01.xls.
2. The migration to the Sun Belt stems from a wide variety of sources, including the desire of businesses to locate in areas with cheap land and labor. One important influence is the widespread use of air conditioners. It is extremely unlikely that Arizona would now have a population of nearly 6 million if not for air conditioning.
3. For data on the age distribution of the population, see http://www.census.gov/popest/ states/asrh/SC-est2004–02.html.
4. Projections for the age distribution of the population for the 50 states can be found at http://www.census.gov/population/www/projections/statepyramid.html.
5. Since 1970, the Census Bureau has provided population estimates for the years between censuses, and these are used in figure 2.2. For the years before 1970, the data for Detroit's population are taken from the decennial censuses, and the population numbers for the years between censuses in figure 2.2 are interpolated.
6. See Patricia Montemurri, Kathleen Gray, and Cecil Angel, "Detroit Tops Nation in Poverty Census," Detroit Free Press, August 31, 2005, available at http://www.freep.com/news/locway/ poor31e_20050831.htm.
7. Crary, Erickcek, and Goodman focus on the following metropolitan areas: Ann Arbor, Benton Harbor, Detroit, Flint, Grand Rapids–Muskegon–Holland, Jackson, Kalamazoo–Battle Creek, Lansing–East Lansing, and Saginaw–Bay City–Midland.

8. These data are taken from selected issues of the *Statistical Abstract of the United States,* available at *http://www.census.gov/statab/www/*.

9. For an excellent discussion of the changing gender gap, see Francine Blau and Lawrence Kahn, "Gender Differences in Pay," *Journal of Economic Perspectives* 14 (2000): 75–99.

10. For more details, see the population chapter by Kenneth Darga, and the labor-markets chapter by George Johnson, in *Michigan at the Millennium*.

11. A wealth of data on rates of unionization can be found at *http://www.unionstats.com/*. The unionized percentage of the labor force is highest in New York State, where 25.3 percent of workers were union members in 2004. New York is followed by Hawaii, and then Michigan. At the other end of the scale, North Carolina has the smallest proportion of unionized workers, at 2.7 percent.

12. For example, see Thomas Holmes, "The Effects of State Policies on the Location of Industry: Evidence from State Borders," *Journal of Political Economy* 106 (1998): 667–705. The loss of employment among union members can also have spillover effects on the nonunion labor force. If there are job losses among unionized workers, at least some of the displaced workers will then look for work in the nonunion sector of the economy. Since more workers will then be competing for the nonunion jobs, the wages in those jobs can be expected to decrease.

13. In a recent radio interview, *Wall Street Journal* automotive reporter Jeffrey McCracken provided some incisive comments on poor management decisions in the American automobile industry. According to McCracken, "Both GM and Ford, when they were riding high in the mid and late nineties with truck and SUV profits, perhaps that was the time when they needed to truly invest and make themselves both leaner companies at the manufacturing level, so that they could compete with the Asian auto makers, but also should have invested truly in the car side of the business. They in essence trained consumers not to think of them when they thought of cars. 'Think of us when you're looking for a pickup truck. Think of us when you want a big, full-sized SUV. But if you're looking for a fuel-efficient car, well, that's what the Accord and the Camry are for.'" The entire interview from December 2, 2005, is available at *http://www.npr.org/templates/story/story.php?storyId=5036606*.

14. Throughout the U.S. economy, there has been a trend toward huge increases in pay for top executives. In 1982, the chief executive officers (CEOs) of 367 leading U.S. corporations earned an average of 42 times as much as the average production worker. By 1990, the CEOs were making 107 times as much as the production workers. In 2004, CEO pay was 431 times as great as production-worker pay. (See Scott Anderson, John Cavanagh, Scott Klinger, and Liz Stanton, "Executive Excess 2005," available at *http://www.faireconomy.org/press/2005/EE2005.pdf*.)

15. The data in tables 2.2 and 2.3 are from the U.S. Census Bureau, "Educational Attainment in the United States: 2004," table 13, at *http://www.census.gov/population/www/socdemo/education/cps2004.html.*

16. See "Labor Markets and Human Capital Investment in Michigan: Challenges and Strategies," by Rebecca Blank and James Sallee of the University of Michigan, available at *http://closup.umich.edu/research/conferences/wdwgfh/blank.pdf.*

17. Figure 2.3 makes it appear as if the percentage of Michigan residents with a bachelor's degree has bounced up and down a few times in recent years. This probably reflects the fact that the census data shown in figure 2.3 are based on a sample, rather than on the entire population. If we had information from a larger sample, the fluctuations shown in figure 2.3 would probably be smoothed out.

18. Every year, I teach a course in introductory microeconomics to large numbers of students at Michigan State University. The overwhelming majority of my students went to high schools in Michigan. The best of these students are outstanding, but far too many have serious deficiencies, especially in mathematics. Some data on the extent of the problem can be found in Charles Ballard and Marianne Johnson, "Basic Math Skills and Performance in an Introductory Economics Class," *Journal of Economic Education* 35 (2004): 3–23.

19. These data are from the Current Population Survey. They can be found on the web site of the Bureau of the Census, at *http://pubdb3.census.gov/macro/032005/perinc/new03_000.htm.*

20. These data were taken from the website of the Bureau of Labor Statistics, at *http://stats.bls.gov/news.release/empsit.t04.htm.*

21. See Timothy Bartik, "Increasing the Economic Development Benefits of Higher Education in Michigan," Upjohn Institute Staff Working Paper No. 04-106, September 27, 2004, available at *http://www.upjohninst.org/publications/wp/04–106.pdf.*

22. See Claudia Goldin, "Egalitarianism and the Returns to Education during the Great Transformation of American Education," *Journal of Political Economy* 107 (1999): S65-S94.

23. The Chicago Fed (Federal Reserve Bank of Chicago) serves the Seventh Federal Reserve District, which includes the Lower Peninsula of Michigan, as well as all of Iowa and parts of Illinois, Indiana, and Wisconsin.

24. The data for figure 2.4 are from table 247 of the Digest of Education Statistics, 2004, at *http://nces.ed.gov/programs/digest/d04/tables/dt04_247.asp.* More generally, the website of the National Center for Education Statistics, at *http://nces.ed.gov*, has a huge wealth of information on a wide variety of topics.

25. This problem of limited productivity gains is sometimes known as the "Baumol Disease," after the economist William J. Baumol (see Baumol, "Macroeconomics of Unbalanced Growth: The Anatomy of Urban Crisis," *American Economic Review* 57 [1967]: 415–426). The

problem is even more serious in the arts than in education. A performance of Beethoven's Symphony No. 9 will take a few hundred performers, and it will take about 65 minutes. If anyone were to attempt to "improve productivity" by using fewer performers and cutting the time of the performance, the results would be very unsatisfactory.

26. These data are from table 78 of the Digest of Education Statistics, 2004, available at *http://nces.ed.gov/programs/digest/d04/tables/dt04_078.asp*.

27. See table 68 of the 2004 Digest of Education Statistics, at *http://nces.ed.gov/programs/digest/d04/tables/dt04_068.asp*.

28. The data for these calculations, along with a tremendous amount of additional information, can be found in "School Finance Reform in Michigan: Proposal A: A Retrospective," prepared by the Office of Revenue and Tax Analysis of the Michigan Department of Treasury in December 2002. This report is available at *http://www.michigan.gov/documents/propa_3172_7.pdf*.

29. See Leslie E. Papke, "The Effects of Spending on Test Pass Rates: Evidence from Michigan," *Journal of Public Economics* 89 (2005): 821–839.

30. See David Arsen, Tom Clay, Thomas Davis, Thomas Devaney, Rachel Fulcher-Dawson, and David N. Plank, "Adequacy, Equity, and Capital Spending in Michigan Schools: The Unfinished Business of Proposal A" (issued May 2005), available at *http://www.crcmich.org/PUBLICAT/2000s/2005/schoolcapital.pdf*.

31. Here I have argued against complete equalization of per-pupil expenditures across the state. A similar story can be told for the distribution of income in general. The distribution of income has become substantially less equal in the last three decades, and I argue in this book for policies that will restore more equality. However, I certainly do not advocate complete leveling of incomes. If all incomes were equal, the incentive to work, save, and invest would be destroyed, and the overall level of economic activity would be drastically reduced.

32. The pension plan for Michigan teachers is a prefunded plan, which means that real assets are accumulated over time. However, it is also a "defined-benefit" plan. This means that if the investment portfolio's performance is subpar, additional contributions have to be made in order to reach a prespecified level of retirement-benefit payments. Thus, the investment risk is borne by the taxpayers. This stands in contrast to a "defined-contribution" plan, under which investment risk is borne by the beneficiaries. Examples of defined-contribution plans include 401(k) plans and the TIAA-CREF system that serves most college teachers. Defined-benefit plans can quickly become underfunded, whereas defined-contribution plans are always fully funded, by definition. This is one of the reasons for the growing popularity of defined-contribution plans. For example, after 1997, newly hired state

employees were no longer eligible for a defined-benefit plan. Instead, they were given access to a defined-contribution plan. For more discussion of these issues, see "Public Pensions and Pension Policy in Michigan," by Leslie Papke of Michigan State University, in *Michigan at the Millennium*.

33. See Citizens Research Council of Michigan, Report 337, "Financing Michigan Retired Teacher Pension and Health Care Benefits," September 2004, available at *http://www.crcmich.org/PUBLICAT/2000s/2004/rpt337.pdf*. Additional discussion of retirement benefits for teachers and other public employees can be found in the *Michigan at the Millennium* chapter by Leslie Papke.

34. The pension benefits are protected by a provision of the Michigan Constitution, but the health benefits do not have any such protection. Thus, if there are reductions in benefits, they may be concentrated in the area of health benefits. Of course, the Constitution could be amended, in which case benefit reductions could occur for pensions as well as for health care.

35. Many of the students in my classes finance their education partly by working long hours during the school year, but this is a very unsatisfactory solution. A student who is working 35 hours per week during the school year may be able to limp through to graduation, but he or she will not be able to derive the full benefits of a college education. If financial aid is reduced far enough, many students from families of modest means will find that a college education is out of reach, regardless of how many hours they might work during the school year.

36. See Alan B. Krueger, "Reassessing the View That American Schools Are Broken," Working Paper No. 395, Industrial Relations Section, Princeton University, January 1998.

37. Another problem, in some school districts, is the proliferation of "half-days," during which school is only in session for a few hours. If the school year is lengthened, it would be important to avoid an offsetting increase in the number of half-days.

38. See Joshua D. Angrist and Alan B. Krueger, "Does Compulsory School Attendance Affect Schooling and Earnings?" *Quarterly Journal of Economics* 106 (1991): 979–1014.

39. A very interesting discussion along these lines can be found in "Graduation Requirements, Skills, Postsecondary Education, and the Michigan Economy," by Timothy Bartik and Kevin Hollenbeck of the Upjohn Institute for Employment Research. The Bartik-Hollenbeck paper can be found at *http://www.upjohninst.org/Bartik-Hollenbeck_testimony.pdf*.

Michigan's Physical Resources: Transportation, Land, and Environment

C hapter 2 was concerned with Michigan's *human* resources. In this chapter, we turn to Michigan's *physical* resources. We begin with a discussion of the transportation system, with special emphasis on highway construction and maintenance. Later in the chapter, we consider the closely related issues of land use and the environment.

Michigan's Transportation System

If you drive very much in Michigan, you probably know the feeling—many of our roads are bone-jarring, teeth-rattling nightmares. It is not just that the roads in Michigan are poor in an absolute sense; they also are not as good as the roads in neighboring states. Kenneth Boyer of Michigan State University discusses Michigan's transportation system in detail in *Michigan at the Millennium*. Although Boyer discusses various aspects of the system, including air, water, and rail transportation, the major focus is on the roads. That is as it should be, since automobile and truck travel account for such a large part of the travel that occurs in Michigan.

Rough Roads and the Policies That Encourage Them

Boyer presents data from the Federal Highway Administration for the percentage of roads that meet various standards for roughness, for the year 2000. Michigan's rural interstate highways are far worse than the rural interstates in the United States as a whole, or in the other states of the Great Lakes region. The same is true for every type of major road in urban areas, including interstate highways, non-interstate freeways, and other arterial highways. The worst roads of all are the non-freeway arterial highways in urban areas.

On the other hand, minor arterial roads in rural areas are somewhat better in Michigan than in the rest of the United States, or the rest of the Great Lakes region. Thus, only the most lightly traveled roads are as good in Michigan as in the rest of the country. In Michigan, the roads that carry a few hundred vehicles per day are likely to be in pretty good shape, but the roads that carry tens of thousands of vehicles per day are likely to be poor.

These data suggest a few questions that need to be answered. First, why are Michigan highways of generally poor quality? Second, why are the most lightly traveled rural roads relatively better than other roads? One possibility is that the people of Michigan drive more, but the evidence does not support this. Another possibility is that Michigan spends less money on roads than other states do, but this does not appear to be the case either.

Instead, it appears that much of the problem comes from the way in which Michigan allocates its road dollars. Highway funds in Michigan are allocated on the basis of formulas that were developed many years ago. These formulas are extraordinarily biased in favor of rural counties. Under the formulas, the most heavily populated county in the state (Wayne County) gets less than $40 per person for its roads every year, while sparsely populated Schoolcraft County gets more than $1,000 per person per year.

The pattern of road ownership in Michigan is also unusual. Federal funds are used for major highways, but not for local streets and roads. Thus, generally speaking, the most heavily traveled highways are the federal-aid highways. In most states, the state highway agency owns most of the federal-aid highways. In Michigan's case, the state highway authority is the Michigan Department of Transportation (MDOT). However, the fraction of Michigan's federal-aid highways owned by MDOT is only about half as large as the fraction of such highways in other states that are owned by those states' highway authorities. Instead, county road commissions own well over half of these major highways in Michigan.

This pattern of ownership may have an effect on the decisions made about what kinds of roads to build. It is possible that the county road commissions face a different political environment, and that this contributes to the relatively high quality of minor rural highways in Michigan when compared to the more heavily traveled roads.[1]

Michigan also allows much heavier trucks than are allowed in most other states. The gross weight limit on trucks in Michigan is more than twice as heavy as the limit imposed on federal-aid highways in some states. (Michigan was allowed to keep its higher weight limits, based on laws from the 1960s.) It is hard to ignore the apparent relationship between two facts: (1) Michigan allows unusually heavy trucks to travel on its highways, and (2) Michigan's highways are unusually poor. Kenneth Boyer discusses this issue in *Michigan at the Millennium*. As it turns out, there is not enough scientific evidence to reach a definite conclusion as to whether ultraheavy trucks cause excessive damage to the roads. More engineering studies could help to improve our understanding of the effect of ultraheavy trucks on road quality. Until more studies are available, of course, no one is suggesting that ultraheavy trucks are *beneficial* to the roads.

Thus, it appears that there are some strong connections between road *policies* and road *quality*. In other words, we in Michigan have chosen to have crummy roads because we have chosen policies that lead to crummy roads. This discussion suggests three possible policy changes that could help to improve the quality of Michigan's highways. The first and foremost is to change the formula by which state funds are allocated to the counties. The current formula shows a huge bias in favor of thinly populated rural counties. As a result, Michigan's road dollars are misallocated, with too much money going to areas that do not need as much, and too little money going to the areas with greatest need. By reducing the discrimination against urban counties, it will be possible for Michigan to improve many roads that are both heavily traveled and of poor quality, without spending any additional money.

The second policy change would give the Michigan Department of Transportation greater control over the major highways in the state. If the MDOT were in charge of a larger percentage of the state's highways, it might be possible to allocate the state's road resources in a more efficient manner. Once again, this change might make it possible to improve the overall quality of Michigan's highways without spending any additional money.

The third policy change would reduce the weight limits on trucks in Michigan. As suggested above, we do not have absolutely definitive evidence that the ultraheavy trucks allowed in Michigan cause disproportionate road damage. Nevertheless, a reduction in the weight limits is worth considering. Regardless of whether the truck weight limits are changed in the near future, it would make sense to engage in research to increase our knowledge about the effect of ultraheavy trucks on road quality. Additional research could provide a more solid factual foundation on which to base future policies.

Road Finance

In the previous section, we emphasized ways to improve the roads in Michigan without spending additional money. This could be accomplished by reallocating the money currently spent on road construction and repair, and by reducing the stress on the roads from ultraheavy trucks. However, even if policies change along these lines, Michigan's road problems will still not be solved entirely. Michigan's roads are in such bad shape that it will require more money to get our road system into acceptable condition. Thus, in this section, we turn our attention to the sources of funds for road construction and repair.

In Michigan, as in the rest of the United States, most of the money for road construction and road repair comes from sources that can be thought of as "user fees." These include fuel taxes, registration fees, and tolls. Most of the funding for roads in Michigan comes from taxes and fees collected in Michigan, but about one-fourth of the total comes from the federal government. (However, the amount that Michigan receives from the Federal Highway Trust Fund has historically been less than the amount of the state's payments into the fund.)

Michigan is unusual in its generosity toward users of diesel fuel. In most states, the diesel tax is at least as large as the tax on gasoline. Also, the federal diesel tax is higher than the federal gasoline tax. In Michigan, however, the tax on gasoline is 19 cents per gallon, and the tax on diesel fuel is 15 cents per gallon.[2] There is no clear reason why diesel motorists should receive this privileged treatment. Michigan should raise the tax rate on diesel fuel, at least to parity with the gasoline tax. Beyond that, increases in both the diesel tax and the gasoline tax would provide additional funds for highway construction and maintenance.[3]

All around the globe, road construction and maintenance are increasingly being paid for by modern toll-collection systems, such as "EZ-Pass." Tolls can raise a substantial amount of revenue, and they can also help to relieve congestion. Larger tolls can be used in the most heavily congested areas. Also, tolls can be reduced or eliminated at off-peak times of the day and week, and increased during the periods of heaviest traffic. When tolls are adjusted in this manner, they will encourage drivers to drive during off-peak times, thus spreading out the volume of traffic across the day and week. Effectively, this increases the capacity of the roads.

Despite these advantages of tolls, they have never been popular in Michigan. Other states use tolls far more than Michigan. But there is no reason for Michigan to shy away from the use of tolls. They can raise revenue for maintaining the roads, and they can help us to use the existing roads in a more efficient manner.

Public Transportation

So far, this section has concentrated exclusively on roads. Thus, the implied emphasis has been on transportation using private passenger automobiles, since most road traffic involves private cars. However, potentially at least, the people of Michigan could use public transportation. I say "potentially" because Michigan residents do not actually use public transportation very much. In *Michigan at the Millennium*, Kenneth Boyer compares public-transportation usage in various metropolitan areas in the Midwest. He finds that public transportation is far less prevalent in the Detroit area and the Grand Rapids area than would be expected for metropolitan areas of their size. Detroit is the second-largest metropolitan area in the region, but the people in the Detroit area use public transportation far less than those in the Chicago area (which is the largest in the Midwest) or in the Cleveland area (which is third-largest). The big difference between Detroit and Chicago or Cleveland is that Detroit lacks a significant rail-transit system.

We in Michigan do not use public transportation very much. Should we? As usual in economics, the answer to the question depends on our estimates of the benefits and costs. Public-transportation systems cost money. Boyer emphasizes that public systems usually cover only a small fraction of their operating expenses, which means that these systems have to receive government subsidies.

On the other hand, the true social costs of automobile driving are probably far greater than the costs borne privately by individual drivers. In making the decision about whether to drive, an individual motorist will only take into account the private operating costs of driving. The individual motorist does not take into account the external costs that he or she imposes on the rest of society, in the form of traffic congestion, air pollution, and noise.[4]

The benefits of public transportation are somewhat different for rail systems and bus systems. Rail systems can encourage denser patterns of residential and commercial development, which may have advantages. (Later in this chapter, we will return to the issue of the density of development.) Bus systems can provide access to transportation for low-income people and others who are unable to travel by passenger automobile. In the long run, one possible advantage of both bus and rail systems is that they would reduce the need to pave over large sections of our downtowns for parking lots.

Clearly, major investments in public transportation are not appropriate in all parts of the state. For the foreseeable future, most travel in most parts of Michigan will continue to occur in private passenger automobiles. However, a case can be made for a rail transit system in the Detroit metropolitan area. From the perspective of Michigan, the case for a rail system could depend partly on who pays for it. In the past, the federal government has paid a substantial portion of the capital expenses for many public-transportation projects. If this were to occur for a rail-transit system in the Detroit area, it would reduce the costs for the people of Michigan.

As this book is being written, the price of oil is above $70 per barrel. The price of gasoline is almost $3 per gallon in much of Michigan, and prices in excess of $3 per gallon have become commonplace in some parts of the country. If the price of gasoline continues to rise, people will respond in a variety of ways. Some folks who have never been part of a carpool may decide to give it a try. Some may shop for more fuel-efficient vehicles. And some may become more interested in public transit. At this point, there does not seem to be much of a public clamor for increased investment in public transportation. However, if the price of gasoline stays high enough for long enough, we may see increased interest in public transportation. For an excellent discussion of these and other aspects of transportation in Michigan, see the chapter in *Michigan at the Millennium* by Kenneth Boyer.

Land Use

In chapter 1 of this book, we looked at Michigan's population trends. The population of Michigan grew very rapidly in the middle of the twentieth century, but the growth rate slowed down dramatically after 1970. If the population growth rate had been the same after 1970 as it was between 1940 and 1970, Michigan would have about 5 million more people today than it actually has. Lots of people in Michigan view the sluggish growth of our economy and population as a cause for concern. However, it should be recognized that there is a positive aspect to the slower growth: More people in Michigan would have meant more pressure on Michigan's land. It probably would have meant that more farms and forests would have been covered over with houses, stores, offices, roads, and parking lots.

The situation in Michigan stands in dramatic contrast to the situation in California. In 1960, California had about 15.7 million people. By 1984, California's population had risen to about 25.8 million, and it had risen to about 35.8 million by 2004.⁵ Thus, between 1960 and 1984, the *growth* of California's population was as large as the *entire* Michigan population today. And then, between 1984 and 2004, California gained *another* Michigan population. Consequently, the attitude toward growth is very different in the two states. In Michigan, there is a strong desire to attract more businesses, more economic activity, and more people. On the other hand, people just keep flooding into California. The focus in California is very much on how to manage and control the growth, and not so much on stimulating additional growth.

Despite the differences between Michigan and California, there are important similarities. Even though the total size of Michigan's population has not grown very rapidly, it is still true that the *geographical distribution* of the population has changed a great deal. In particular, Michigan has shared in the nationwide trend toward suburbanization and lower-density development.

Gary Sands of Wayne State University discusses land-use issues in *Michigan at the Millennium*. Another valuable resource for those interested in land-use issues is "Michigan's Land, Michigan's Future: Final Report of the Michigan Land Use Leadership Council." This report, issued in August 2003, is available at *http://www.michiganlanduse.org/MLULC_FINAL_REPORT_0803.pdf.*

Land Use: Facts and Trends

About 79 percent of the land in Michigan is privately owned, with another 12 percent owned by the State of Michigan, and 9 percent owned by the federal government. In the nonfederal lands in 1997, about one-half was forested, and one-third was used for crops or pasture. Only 10.7 percent of the land was developed in 1997. (This was up from 8.3 percent in 1982.)

One of the most important land-use trends, both nationally and in Michigan, is toward reduced density of development in metropolitan areas. All of the metropolitan areas in Michigan experienced substantial increases in the amount of urbanized land area in the 1980s and 1990s, even though the populations of these areas grew fairly slowly. As a result, population density decreased in the metropolitan areas. For example, from 1982 to 1997 in the Lansing area, population grew by 6.8 percent, but urbanized land area grew by more than 50 percent! As a result, the population density declined by about 29 percent. For the entire United States, urban population density decreased by 20.5 percent during this period. Density decreased more rapidly in some areas in Michigan, and less rapidly in others, but the trend toward decreasing density was seen in every metropolitan area in Michigan.

The trend toward low-density development is not due to any one single cause, but one that deserves mentioning is the price of gasoline. For most of the years since the middle 1980s, gasoline has been relatively inexpensive. This has encouraged low-density development because many people have been able to commute long distances. It remains to be seen whether the recent increases in gasoline prices will be maintained. However, if the price of gasoline does remain relatively high, long-distance commuting will become less attractive. This could encourage some movement back toward the center of metropolitan areas, although there could also be an increase in the number of people who engage in telecommuting.

A possible advantage of low-density development is that it allows people to fulfill the "American Dream" of a big house on a large lot. However, low-density development also causes problems. One of the problems is increased congestion in the suburbs. In *Michigan at the Millennium*, Gary Sands presents evidence of the growing level of suburban congestion. Another problem is loss of open space. A third problem comes in the form of increased costs of infrastructure, as water, sewer services, and electricity have to be provided to distant regions. Sands reports the results of a 1997 study carried out for the Southeast Michigan Council of Governments. The study found that compact, higher-density growth leads to reduced needs for infrastructure. This, in turn, has a positive fiscal effect on local governments.

Selected Land-Use Policies

One problem identified by Sands is that land use in Michigan has traditionally been characterized by a lack of planning and coordination. It was against this background that "Michigan's Land, Michigan's Future" was written by the Michigan Land Use Leadership Council in 2003. This report contains dozens of recommendations, and it is far too detailed to summarize here. But the report and the process that produced it show an increased recognition of the need for a rational and organized set of land-use policies in Michigan.

Out of the hundreds of issues relevant to land-use policy, I have selected a few for special comment here:

• *Open space.* In 1974, Michigan passed Public Law 116, which allows owners of agricultural lands to apply for a development-rights agreement. Under such an agreement, the owner agrees not to develop the property, in return for a reduction in property taxes. I do not want to speak in opposition to the preservation of agricultural land as such. However, policy discussions in this area sometimes make it sound as if preservation of agricultural land and preservation of open space are identical. They are not.

There is nothing wrong with privately owned agricultural land. However, from the perspective of the vast majority of Michigan residents who live in metropolitan areas, parks may be more valuable than farms. One of the most distinctive features of the urban landscape in the entire United States is Manhattan's Central Park. This huge green rectangle contributes immeasurably to the character and quality of life of America's largest city. In fact, however, parts of what is now Central Park were once farmland. If enough subsidies had been provided to the farmers, Central Park might still be a farm, instead of a park. And yet I doubt whether the people of New York City would be better off if Central Park were an alfalfa farm instead of a park. Again, I want to stress that this is not a diatribe against agriculture. Instead, I am trying to raise an issue that is likely to become more and more important over time in Michigan. Future population growth in Michigan is likely to be concentrated in the metropolitan areas of the southern Lower Peninsula. The future residents of these areas will benefit from open space, and not merely from open space in the form of farms. Now is the time to devote planning and financial resources to making sure that future generations of Michigan residents have sufficient amounts of convenient parks and recreational facilities. Note that the financial resources for these facilities do not necessarily have to come from public sources. State and local governments should be ready and willing to work constructively with private donors who express an interest in providing funds for such facilities.

• *The tax system's incentives for sprawl.* In 1978, the voters of Michigan passed the "Headlee Amendment" to the Michigan Constitution. The Headlee Amendment placed restrictions on the property taxes that could be levied by jurisdictions in the state. Under certain circumstances, the Headlee Amendment can trigger an automatic reduction in the property-tax millage rate. However, the law also allowed for ways to avoid the restrictions. In particular, new construction is excluded from the Headlee calculations. This means that rapidly growing communities (which are more likely to be in the distant suburbs) are more likely to be able to avoid a "Headlee Rollback." Older cities, which tend to grow less rapidly, are more likely to bump into the restrictions.

Most of the voters who approved the Headlee Amendment probably did so because of their desire to limit property taxes. My guess is that few of the voters saw it as a mechanism for encouraging suburban sprawl. And yet it appears that suburban sprawl may have been an unintended byproduct of the Headlee Amendment. The Headlee Amendment has helped to perpetuate the inequalities in tax and spending levels that existed in Michigan in 1978.[6]

What, if anything, should be done? The Headlee Amendment is only one piece of a broader set of policies, and so it would be inappropriate to focus too narrowly on the Amendment. In general, however, it would be wise for Michigan to develop a comprehensive strategy to put older developed areas on an even footing with newly developing areas.

• *Reinvigorating Michigan's cities.* In chapter 1 of this book, I described how the population of Detroit has fallen by about *one million* in the last 50 years.

There is plenty of space for redevelopment in Detroit. Any rational strategy for land use in southeast Michigan would recognize the benefits of using the land throughout the region, including the land in Detroit.

In chapter 1, and elsewhere, I have also described the huge increase in inequality, which has been one of the most important features of the economic landscape in America in the last 30 years. Not everyone who lives in a city is poor, and not everyone who lives in a suburb is affluent, but the suburbs do tend to be richer than the cities. As the gap between rich and poor has widened, so has the gap between suburb and city.

In chapter 2 of this book, I described the difficulties facing school districts with low levels of taxable property per student. Although local school districts do not have to depend on local property taxes for their *operating* expenses, they do have to rely almost exclusively on local property taxes for their *capital* expenditures. This means that many of the older urban districts are unable to provide adequate school facilities, even if they impose high tax rates. This can only exacerbate the flight to the suburbs and further weaken the cities.

Earlier in this chapter, I described the astonishing inequity in the formula for allocating state transportation funds. Urban counties receive far fewer dollars per resident than rural counties.

I hope the pattern is clear: Again and again, we see an economic playing field that is tilted against the cities. Almost by definition, cities tend to be developed more densely than suburbs and rural areas. Thus, economic policies to strengthen the cities will tend to lead to more compact development. If Michigan's cities are strengthened, many of the problems associated with low-density land use will be reduced, regardless of what other land-use policies might be undertaken. I do not claim that it will be easy politically to strengthen the cities, but I do believe it will be good policy.

For those interested in land-use policy, Gary Sands's chapter in *Michigan at the Millennium* is highly recommended, as is "Michigan's Land, Michigan's Future" cited above.

Environment

I have divided this chapter into three sections—on transportation, land use, and now on the environment. This division is clearly somewhat arbitrary. The lines between transportation, land use, and the environment are often blurry. For example, low-density development is not merely a land-use issue. It is also an environmental issue, because low-density development is associated with destruction of wildlife habitat, as well as other pressures on the ecosystem. Nevertheless, in this section, we now move on to a fuller discussion of environmental issues.

Increased Environmental Awareness

In *Michigan at the Millennium*, environmental issues are discussed by Gloria Helfand of the University of Michigan, and John Wolfe of Limno-Tech, Inc. (formerly of Michigan State University). They describe some of the changes in the last few decades, both in environmental policy and in the quality of the environment. Prior to the 1960s, environmental concerns were low on America's list of priorities. However, environmental awareness increased substantially in the late 1960s and early 1970s. In 1968, Michigan voters passed a bond measure for the purpose of cleaning the state's waters. In 1970, the federal government passed the Clean Air Act and authorized the Environmental Protection Agency, and Michigan passed the Michigan Environmental Protection Act. The U.S.-Canada Great Lakes Water Quality Agreement followed in 1972, setting the goal of reducing phosphorus levels in the Lakes. In 1976, Michigan became the first major industrial state to approve a deposit-refund system for beer and pop containers. With a deposit of ten cents per container, the incentive to recycle these containers is stronger in Michigan than in any other state. Over the last few decades, many communities have also established curbside and drop-off recycling programs for newspapers, corrugated cardboard, glass containers, tin cans, and a variety of other materials. The "Superfund" law, passed in 1980, has led to better handling of hazardous substances, and to cleanup of some hazardous-waste sites, although many sites remain. In 1998, Michigan voters passed the $675 million Clean Michigan Initiative. Thus, we now have nearly 40 years of heightened awareness of environmental concerns, matched by a wide variety of policies designed to create a cleaner environment.

Trends in Environmental Quality: Air, Water, and Wetlands

Not all of the policies mentioned in the previous paragraph have been equally successful. On balance, however, considerable progress has been made. In many ways, the environment of Michigan and the environment of the rest of the United States are much improved since 1970. Because of laws requiring unleaded gasoline, lead levels in the atmosphere have decreased dramatically. Emissions of carbon monoxide, particulate matter, and volatile organic compounds have dropped since the 1980s, although emissions of nitrous oxides have increased.

The amount of phosphorus entering Lake Erie decreased by more than 80 percent between 1972 and 1982. As a result, the growth of algae in Lake Erie has been reduced very substantially, and fish populations have returned. However, uncontrolled discharges of nitrogen and phosphorus still do occur. In 1998, nearly 5 percent of Michigan's lakes were classified as hypereutrophic (i.e., characterized by excessive amounts of algae and other plant life). Nearly 300 beach closings were reported in a survey in 2000.

Helfand and Wolfe report that during the first 200 years of U.S. history, the lower 48 states lost about 53 percent of their wetlands. Michigan is close to the national average, with a loss of about half its wetlands. On the other hand, Illinois, Indiana, and Ohio lost more than 85 percent of their original wetlands because these states engaged in much more drainage for farmland. In the last 20 years, policy initiatives have sought to reduce the loss of wetlands. Helfand and Wolfe present evidence that these policies have been partly successful: the rate of wetland loss has slowed down considerably.

Solid Waste and Landfill

One effect of recycling programs is to reduce the demand for landfill, because the recycled materials are no longer being thrown away. In addition, in 1993 Michigan banned landfilling of yard waste. These changes led to excess landfill capacity in Michigan. This, in turn, put downward pressure on landfill prices, which has probably played a role in attracting imports of waste from other states and Canada.

Imported waste, especially imported waste from Canada, has generated a lot of policy discussion in Michigan. Before we blame too many of our problems on the Canadians, however, it is good to have some perspective on the amount of trash that comes into Michigan from Canada. In 2001, about 80 percent of the solid waste that went to landfill in Michigan was from Michigan. About 10 percent was from Canada, 4 percent from Illinois, 3 percent from Indiana, 2 percent from Ohio, and 1 percent from Wisconsin. Thus, if solid waste from Canada were eliminated completely, landfills in Michigan would still be receiving about 90 percent as much waste as they receive now. If we were to eliminate all solid waste from all sources outside Michigan, landfills in Michigan would still be receiving about 80 percent as much waste as they receive now.

The United States Constitution prohibits the individual states from interfering with international trade. Thus, Michigan cannot restrict imports of waste from Canada unless the federal government intervenes. The Michigan Legislature has indicated its willingness to restrict these imports, if Congress agrees. At this point, it is difficult to say how the issue will be resolved. I am not against regulation of solid waste as such. There is a role for government in regulating solid waste, to make sure that hazardous materials are treated properly. Thus, if restrictions are imposed on solid waste from Canada, there may be some beneficial effects. But it is important to keep things in perspective, and to understand that restrictions on Canadian trash will not solve everything. The vast majority of trash that goes into Michigan landfills is from Michigan sources. Pound for pound, Michigan trash is likely to have environmental effects that are very similar to the effects of Canadian trash. If the people of Michigan want to reduce the amount of solid waste that goes to landfill, the biggest strides can be made through reducing the amount of stuff that gets thrown away by the residents of Michigan.

Cleaning Up Contaminated Sites: How Good Is Good Enough?

The original goal of Michigan's Environmental Response Act was "to eliminate environmental contamination." Unfortunately, cleaning up contaminated soil and groundwater is technically very challenging. As reported by Helfand and Wolfe, studies in the early 1990s suggested that there were more than 300,000 groundwater contamination sites in the United States, and that the cost of cleaning them up might be as high as $1 trillion.

As scientists have learned more about the daunting technical difficulties of cleaning up subsurface contamination, the policy goal has become more modest. It is now recognized that complete elimination of environmental contamination may be impossible, or at least prohibitively expensive. At many sites, the best that can be done is to contain the contamination while engaging in more research to try to find better ways of cleaning up. Thus, the emphasis has changed from the unrealistic goal of eliminating contamination to the more realistic goal of managing risk. In the words of Helfand and Wolfe, "The challenge is to identify sites with the greatest risks and to find cost-effective, permanent means of reducing those risks." (448). For discussion of these and a host of other environmental issues, the chapter in *Michigan at the Millennium* by Helfand and Wolfe is highly recommended.

The Need for Environmental Policy Coordination

One theme that has come up repeatedly in this book is that Michigan is closely interconnected with the rest of the United States, and the rest of the world. This is every bit as true in the environmental area as in any other aspect of our lives. Air pollutants travel with wind currents across state lines and national borders. Invasive species can travel on ship hulls, or in ballast, or under their own power. Contaminated ground water can flow far from its original source. All of these issues point to the need for greater coordination among the regions of the state, and among the states, and between the United States and other countries.

No issue is more international in scope than global warming due to greenhouse gases. A ton of carbon dioxide that goes into the upper atmosphere from Michigan will have about the same ultimate effect on the climate as a ton of carbon dioxide from Wisconsin, or Texas, or Germany, or China. There is much controversy in the scientific literature about how much we can expect global temperatures to rise in the next century. There are even a few who dispute whether global warming is an issue at all, but these folks are an increasingly small minority. In recent years, the scientific community has reached more and more of a consensus that global warming is already underway, and that it will continue. The only real controversy is over how hot it will get.

What can we in Michigan do about global warming? We can plant trees. We can drive fewer miles, and we can drive in more fuel-efficient vehicles. But because of the global nature of the problem, the actions of Michigan residents will have to be a part of a much broader national and international campaign. It remains to be seen whether national and world leaders will have the wisdom and courage necessary to make a serious effort to reduce emissions of greenhouse gases.

Conclusion

In this chapter, we have discussed some aspects of the physical environment in Michigan. We began with a look at the transportation system, with special emphasis on the quality of our roads. We then considered land-use issues, followed by other environmental issues. Here are some of the highlights:

- With the exception of minor highways in rural areas, Michigan's roads are of significantly worse quality than the roads in the rest of the United States, or the rest of the Great Lakes region. All categories of urban roads are worse in Michigan than elsewhere. Thus, ironically, Michigan's lightly traveled rural roads are the only ones that are likely to be of comparable quality to those in neighboring states. If a road in Michigan serves tens of thousands of motorists every day, it is likely to be of poorer quality than a similar road in other states.

- A number of policies have an influence on the poor quality of Michigan's roads. The most important of these is the misallocation of state highway funds. The spending formula devotes hugely disproportionate amounts of money to sparsely populated rural counties. As a result, the more densely populated urban counties have less money for roads. A new formula, devoting relatively more money to urban areas, would be both more equitable and more efficient. Another policy issue has to do with ownership of the major highways. The Michigan Department of Transportation owns relatively few of the major roads, whereas county road commissions own the lion's share. The heavy tilt toward county road commissions may also contribute to the fact that Michigan's lightly traveled rural roads are relatively better than its urban highways.

- Truck weight limits are far higher in Michigan than in the rest of the country. There is not enough scientific evidence to say for certain whether this contributes to the poor quality of roads in Michigan. However, it is certainly possible that ultraheavy trucks do an unusually large amount of damage to the roads.

- Currently, Michigan's tax on diesel fuel is 15 cents per gallon, which is four cents per gallon lower than the gasoline tax. In most states, on the other hand, the diesel tax is equal to or greater than the gasoline tax. There is no good reason to favor diesel users in this way. The diesel tax should be increased so that it is at least equal to the gasoline tax. Moreover, even though some of the reforms mentioned above would improve Michigan's roads without an overall increase in spending, the condition of the roads is such that it will be necessary to increase the total amount of funding for road construction and repair. Additional revenue could be obtained by increasing the tax rates on both gasoline and diesel fuel.

• Tolls can raise revenue for road construction and maintenance. Also, if tolls are varied according to the time of day and the day of the week, they can help to spread out the volume of traffic, thus increasing the effective capacity of the existing roads. Michigan has never made substantial use of tolls, but greater use of tolls should be actively considered.

• Unlike the Chicago area or the Cleveland area, the Detroit area does not have a rail-transit system. As a result, Michigan's use of public transportation is much less than the average in the Great Lakes region, or in the United States as a whole.

• In Michigan, as in the rest of the United States, population density in metropolitan areas has been decreasing. Low-density development is associated with increased congestion in the suburbs, loss of open space, and increased infrastructure costs.

• The "Headlee Amendment" restricts the ability of local jurisdictions to levy property taxes. However, new construction is excluded from the Headlee calculations. Thus, the Headlee Amendment indirectly encourages growth in outlying areas. In fact, the Headlee Amendment is only one of several policies in Michigan that favor sparsely populated and/or newly developing areas over densely populated and/or older areas.

• Michigan would benefit from the development of a comprehensive strategy to level the playing field between older developed areas and newly developing areas.

• In many ways, the environment in Michigan is in better condition now than it was in 1970. Several categories of air pollution are down, the destruction of wetlands has slowed down, and discharges of phosphorus into lakes and streams have been greatly reduced. Also, far more containers and other materials are recycled now than before. Nevertheless, a significant number of serious environmental challenges remain.

• The increase in recycling had the unintended side effect of leading to excess landfill capacity in Michigan. This helped to keep landfill prices low, and it encouraged imports of solid waste from other states and from

Canada. Depending on the resolution of legal and constitutional issues, Michigan may restrict solid-waste imports from Canada. However, it should be understood that the vast majority of the solid waste deposited in Michigan landfills comes from Michigan.

• Michigan's laws originally had the goal of eliminating environmental contamination. Unfortunately, experience has shown that there are profound technical difficulties in cleaning up contaminated ground water and sediments. It is now recognized that it may be impossible, or at least prohibitively expensive, to clean up all sites completely. The challenge is to identify the sites with the greatest risks, and to find the best methods of reducing those risks.

In this chapter and the previous one, we have often dealt with budgetary issues. In chapter 4, we take a look at the entire budget of the State of Michigan, and we consider some aspects of the budget that have not been emphasized so far, including corrections, health care, and programs for low-income and low-wage workers.

NOTES

1. When compared with neighboring states, Michigan also makes far greater use of unpaved roads.

2. Because of the stop-and-go nature of driving in cities, urban drivers get fewer miles per gallon than rural drivers, but rural and urban drivers pay the gasoline tax at the same rate per gallon. Thus, the tax rate per mile is higher for urban motorists than for their rural counterparts.

3. One odd feature of the taxes on gasoline and diesel fuel (along with the taxes on cigarettes, beer, and wine) is that they are levied on a *per-unit* basis. Most other taxes, including the sales tax, the income tax, and property taxes, are levied as a *percentage* of some dollar value. Because of inflation, the real purchasing power of a unit tax will be reduced over time. The unit taxes could be improved by converting them to the percentage tax that would raise the same amount of revenue. This issue is discussed in detail in chapter 5.

4. For more on the external costs of driving, see Todd Litman, *Transportation Cost Analysis* (Victoria, British Columbia: Victoria Transport Policy Institute, 2002).

5. These population data are taken from various issues of the Statistical Abstract of the United States, available at *http://www.census.gov/statab/www/*.

6. In *Michigan at the Millennium*, an entire chapter (by Susan Fino of Wayne State University) is devoted to the Headlee Amendment. Some of these issues are also discussed in the chapter on the property tax by Naomi Feldman, Paul Courant, and Douglas Drake. In this book, we will return to some of these issues in chapter 5.

Other Budget-Related Issues
and Policies in Michigan

D irectly or indirectly, almost every issue of economic policy in Michigan is affected by the budgets of the state government and local governments. Most chapters in *Michigan at the Millennium* deal with some aspects of government budgets, and two chapters are devoted exclusively to budgetary issues: Gary Olson of the Senate Fiscal Agency gives an overview of state government expenditures, while local government expenditures are discussed by Earl Ryan and Eric Lupher of the Citizens Research Council. In addition, *Michigan at the Millennium* includes a chapter on the fiscal relations among the federal, state, and local governments, by Ronald Fisher of Michigan State University and Jeffrey Guilfoyle of the Office of Revenue and Tax Analysis.

In chapters 2 and 3 of this book, we have already touched on several issues of importance to Michigan's government budgets. Chapter 2 covered education, which is an especially important category of government expenditure in Michigan. The various policy issues discussed in chapter 3 also have implications for the budget. In this chapter, we turn to some other aspects of budget policy. We begin with an overview of the state budget, followed by a discussion of the state's chronic structural budgetary imbalances. We then look at corrections and health care, before turning to programs aimed at low-wage workers, low-income families, and unemployed workers.

The State Budget in Michigan

In table 4.1, we show the total amounts of spending by the various departments and agencies of the state government for the 2006 fiscal year.[1] These
spending categories are ranked by size. The largest is state aid to K–12 education, with nearly $13 billion of expenditures. Community health, which in-
cludes the Medicaid program, is the second-largest category, with about $10.3
billion. These two categories accounted for nearly 56 percent of gross expenditures by the state in fiscal year 2006. Note, however, that not all of these expenditures are actually paid for by Michigan taxpayers. In particular, the
Medicaid program is a joint federal-state program, and the federal government picks up a large portion of Medicaid costs.

Figure 4.1 shows some of the same information that was shown in table 4.1,
but in a different form. The point of figure 4.1 is to show visually that the state
budget is dominated by a relatively small number of expenditure categories.

Spending on the legislature and the executive office account for a total of
only about $135 million, which is less than one-third of one percent of the
state budget. We often hear complaints about the amount spent on elected
officials. However, relative to the rest of the budget, the amounts spent directly on elected officials are a tiny drop in the bucket. If the salaries of legis-
lators, legislative staff, the governor, and the governor's staff were eliminated
completely, the direct effect on the state budget would be negligible.

Structural Budget Deficits

Since the Second World War, the United States economy has experienced 11
recessions. During a typical recession, there is a reduction in employment
and economic activity. As a result, if tax rates do not change, there is also a reduction in tax revenues. Recessions also typically bring an increase in the
number of people seeking social services. The budgetary problems caused by
a recession are known as "cyclical" budgetary pressures, because they are
caused by the business cycle.

The recession of 2001 created cyclical problems for government budgets in
Michigan. However, the budget difficulties faced by today's governments in

TABLE 4.1 Budget for Departments and Agencies of the State of Michigan, Fiscal Year 2006 (Dollar Amounts in Millions)

	AMOUNT	PERCENT OF TOTAL
School Aid	12,757	30.72
Community Health	10,326	24.86
Human Services	4,437	10.68
Transportation	3,388	8.16
Treasury	1,985	4.78
Corrections	1,860	4.48
Universities/Financial Aid	1,734	4.18
Labor and Economic Growth	1,184	2.85
State Police	551	1.33
Management and Budget	505	1.22
Environmental Quality	455	1.10
Information Technology	365	0.88
Community Colleges	281	0.68
Natural Resources	273	0.66
Judiciary	255	0.61
Capital Outlay	228	0.55
Secretary of State	197	0.47
Legislature	130	0.31
Agriculture	119	0.29
Military Affairs	118	0.28
Education	117	0.28
Debt Service	89	0.21
Attorney General	65	0.16
History, Arts, Library	53	0.13
Civil Service	36	0.09
Civil Rights	13	0.03
Executive Office	5	0.01
Total	**41,529**	**100.00**

Source: Office of the State Budget, http://www.michigan.gov/documents/Agency_Budget_schedules_58910_7.pdf.

FIGURE 4.1 Categories of Expenditure in the Budget of the State of Michigan, Fiscal Year 2006

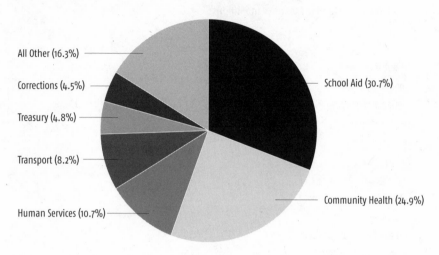

All Other (16.3%)

Corrections (4.5%)

Treasury (4.8%)

Transport (8.2%)

Human Services (10.7%)

School Aid (30.7%)

Community Health (24.9%)

Michigan are *not* fundamentally cyclical in nature—Michigan's budgetary problems continue, even long after the recession is over. Instead, Michigan faces a "structural deficit," which means that the cost of maintaining programs is increasing relative to revenues, even when the economy is expanding.

Every budget has a revenue side and an expenditure side. In Michigan, both sides of the budget have contributed to the structural deficit. On the revenue side, the tax revenues available to Michigan governments have fallen in some recent years, and grown very slowly in other years. The net effect is that the percentage of personal income that goes to state and local governments has been shrinking. The shrinkage has been caused partly by explicit cuts in tax rates, and partly by structural weaknesses in Michigan's major taxes. Consequently, tax revenues in Michigan grow more slowly than the overall economy, even when tax rates remain the same.

We will discuss the tax system in Michigan in much greater detail in chapter 5 of this book. In the current chapter, most of our attention is focused on the expenditure side of the budget.

The Michigan Constitution requires a balanced budget.[2] However, falling tax revenues do not necessarily translate into immediate cuts in programs.

Instead, it may be possible to use up financial reserves (such as the "Rainy Day Fund"), or to make accounting or timing changes (such as the recent change in the timing of property-tax collections). Over the five-year period from 2001 to 2005, Michigan used $6.6 *billion* of these one-time actions.[3]

This extraordinary series of temporary measures made it possible for the state government to support spending at a higher level than could have been supported by recurring tax revenues. However, the day of reckoning could not be postponed forever. As mentioned in chapter 2, education budgets have been cut in recent years, and the pressure on the education budget is expected to rise dramatically in the next 15 years. Many other spending categories have been cut as well.

In the next two sections, we discuss corrections and health care, each of which has had an increasingly large effect on the budget.

Corrections

In the last few decades, the corrections system has been the fastest-growing category of government spending in Michigan. Even after adjusting for inflation, state-government expenditures for corrections were more than four times as large in 2001–2002 as in 1982–1983.[4] The tilt toward corrections has been just as dramatic for the state-government work force. Between 1980 and 2002, corrections employment more than tripled, while employment in all other categories of state government fell by more than one-third. For a detailed discussion of changes in state-government employment, see the opening chapter of *Michigan at the Millennium* by Douglas Drake.

These increases in the corrections budget and work force have been caused primarily by the tremendous increase in the number of inmates. In 1982, some 13,372 prisoners were under the jurisdiction of the State of Michigan. By 2002, this figure had risen to 48,920. In other words, the number of inmates in Michigan was more than 3.6 times as large in 2002 as it had been 20 years earlier.

Michigan's system of criminal justice is discussed in *Michigan at the Millennium*, in a chapter by Sheila Royo Maxwell and Christopher Maxwell of Michigan State University, and David Martin of Wayne State University. They show that prison populations grew very rapidly in the 1980s and 1990s throughout the United States. However, the rate of growth was even faster in Michigan than in most other states. Thus, the prison population per 100,000 residents is higher in Michigan than in the rest of the United States, and substantially higher than in the other states in the Great Lakes region. In large part, this is due to the use of longer prison sentences in Michigan. One result of these sentencing policies is that Michigan's prison population is getting older. In turn, the aging of the prison population means that we can expect further increases in the portion of the corrections budget devoted to health care. Expenditures on health care for prisoners in Michigan are already in excess of $200 million per year.

If the incarceration rate were the same in Michigan as in the other states in the Great Lakes region, prison expenditures in Michigan would be reduced by about $500 million per year.[5] Of course, this does not necessarily mean that Michigan should adopt the less-stringent sentencing policies used in other states. It is possible that the people of Michigan are better off as a result of these incarceration policies. In other words, it is possible that the added expense is worth it in terms of reduced crime. However, in view of the relatively large amount of spending on corrections in Michigan, it makes sense to think very carefully about the benefits and costs of Michigan's corrections policies.

The cost of keeping an inmate in a medium-security prison in Michigan is more than $20,000 per year. Another way to say this is that the annual cost of incarcerating a prisoner is of roughly the same size as the annual cost of sending a student to a good university. Because of these high costs, the criminal-justice system in Michigan has already increased its use of alternatives to incarceration. These include probation, halfway houses, and electronic monitors, as well as other methods of dealing with offenders. In the years to come, Michigan would do well to continue to consider ways to ensure public safety at lower cost. A detailed discussion of these issues can be found in the *Michigan at the Millennium* chapter by Sheila Maxwell, David Martin, and Christopher Maxwell.

Health and Health Care

Governments, companies, and private citizens in the United States spend nearly $2 *trillion* per year on health care. The goal of those expenditures is to improve people's health. Of course, health is affected by many things, and not just by health-care spending. In recent years, Michigan has raised the cigarette tax substantially. This is one of the most important public-health initiatives in Michigan's history, even though it does not show up in the budget as a health-care expenditure.[6] (We will return to the cigarette tax in chapter 5.) Similarly, the population's health will be improved if we can find ways to get Michigan residents to get more exercise and eat a healthier diet, even though this will not have a direct effect on the health-care budget.

As mentioned earlier in this chapter, community health spent more than $10 billion in fiscal year 2006. This would appear to make health care the second-largest category of spending for the State of Michigan. In fact, if we look at the data in a slightly different way, health-care spending is even larger. As discussed in chapter 2, much of the money sent to school districts through the School Aid Fund is actually spent on health care for school employees and retirees. And, as we saw in the preceding section, a substantial amount of the corrections budget is devoted to inmate health care. If we were to put everything associated with health care under one heading, it would be the largest expenditure category of all.

Health and health care in Michigan are discussed in *Michigan at the Millennium* by John Goddeeris of Michigan State University. He shows that the trend toward increased health-care spending has been going on for a very long time, in Michigan and in the rest of the United States. From 1960 to 1993, after adjusting for inflation, real health-care expenditures per person in the United States grew by an astonishing 454 percent. Health-care spending moderated in the middle and late 1990s, but the last several years have brought a new surge of expenditures.

There are many reasons for the trend toward increased health-care expenditure. Part of the increase is a natural result of rising incomes: as American society has become more affluent, the demand for health care has grown rapidly. Changes in medical technology have also played a very large role in the expenditure increases. Some new medical technologies actually lead to cost reductions. (For example, a well-timed dose of antibiotics can be a low-cost way of stopping a sinus infection before it worsens into bronchitis or pneumonia.) But many of the new diagnostic and therapeutic technologies developed in the last generation are very expensive. These new techniques, medicines, and devices have made it possible for the medical profession to provide better care—in many cases, patients have been saved who once would have died. As John Goddeeris points out in *Michigan at the Millennium*, age-adjusted death rates fell substantially in the 1980s and 1990s. Death rates fell at about the same rate in Michigan as in the rest of the country. But the advances did not come cheaply, and future medical advances are also expected to come at a high cost.

Health-care expenditures per person are much higher for elderly people than for younger ones. The elderly will account for an increasingly large percentage of the population in the next few decades, and this will put further upward pressure on health-care spending. In the United States, health expenditures are currently in the vicinity of 16 percent of gross domestic product (GDP). Projections suggest that health expenditures will rise to more than 25 percent of GDP in the next 25 years or so, and that they may eventually rise to 40 percent of GDP, or more.

Public and Private Health-Insurance Coverage

Someone will have to pay for these medical expenditures. In 2004, about 68 percent of the American population had private health-insurance coverage. The vast majority of these people received their coverage through an employer or former employer, or through the employer of a family member. About 27 percent of Americans received health-insurance coverage through government programs (primarily Medicare, which serves elderly and disabled Americans, and Medicaid, which serves low-income children and adults as well as several other categories of beneficiaries). If we add together the 68 percent with private coverage and the 27 percent with government coverage, it might appear that 95 percent of Americans have some sort of coverage. However, some people receive coverage from multiple sources. All told, only about 84 percent of the U.S. population has health insurance.

In Michigan, the proportion with insurance is higher than the national average: in 2004, nearly 89 percent of Michigan residents had some form of health insurance. This is good news. However, if we look at the same data another way, we see that more than one million Michigan residents lack health insurance, along with about 45 million Americans in other states.[7] Among the advanced industrial countries, the United States is unique in having such a large proportion of the population without health insurance.

From the perspective of the Michigan budget, the Medicaid program is by far the most important form of health insurance. Most Medicaid *beneficiaries* are low-income children and adults. However, most Medicaid *expenditures* are for other, more costly groups. These include low-income disabled individuals, low-income elderly people who receive coverage supplementary to Medicare, and elderly people who have exhausted their own ability to pay for long-term care. Both federal and state payments for Medicaid grew very rapidly until the mid-1990s. The rapid growth paused briefly for a few years in the late 1990s, and then took off again in the early years of the twenty-first century. Michigan's payments for Medicaid were about 8 percent of General Fund/General Purpose revenues in 1980. That figure rose to about 17 percent in 1992, and about 25 percent in 2002.

There is every indication that health-care spending will put even more pressure on the budgets of Michigan and the other states, as well as on the federal budget, in the coming years. For example, the federal government spent about $516 billion on Medicare and Medicaid in 2005. According to estimates by the federal Office of Management and Budget, this will increase to about $831 billion by 2011.[8] This is a remarkable growth rate of more than 8 percent per year. Under the current division of responsibility between the federal government and the states, all of the growth of Medicare will fall upon the federal government. But the rapid growth in Medicaid will be shared by Michigan and the other states.

Michigan will have to respond to the pressures created by Medicaid. There are only a few choices for how to do this, and the choices are not easy ones. As John Goddeeris puts it in *Michigan at the Millennium*:

> There are no magic bullets or politically easy answers. Responses must be some combination of the following: (1) Increasing state revenues, which probably implies raising taxes as a share of income in the state; (2) Reallocating revenues from other state priorities to Medicaid; (3) Reducing the number of Medicaid beneficiaries; or (4) Reducing the growth of Medicaid expenditures per beneficiary. (179–80)

Prospects for Fundamental Reform of Health Care

In 1993 and 1994, President Bill Clinton pushed for large-scale reform of the nation's systems of health insurance and health-care delivery. Clinton's efforts were largely unsuccessful, but the issues of health-care reform and health-insurance reform have not gone away. Fundamental reform is far too large a subject to be tackled in depth in a short book like this one. However, a few things deserve to be mentioned.

First, the current medical-insurance system relies very heavily on insurance provided through employers. The people of Michigan and the rest of the United States must face the issue of whether it makes sense for such a large portion of our population to have such a close connection between health insurance and employment. This is of special relevance in Michigan because of the high health-insurance costs of the ailing U.S. automakers. For example, in recent years, General Motors has spent about five and one-half *billion* dollars per year for health coverage for employees, dependents, and retirees.

If we could be certain that companies will march on, year after year, providing health-insurance coverage for their employees from now until forever, then it would make obvious sense to deliver medical insurance through employment. The problem is that companies do not necessarily last forever. Companies are born, and if they are lucky and well managed, they grow. But companies sometimes shrivel, and sometimes die, for a whole host of reasons. As an illustration of this, table 4.2 shows the companies included in the Dow Jones Industrial Average in 1928 (when the Average was first expanded to include 30 companies), and in 2005. Only two of the companies on the list in 1928 still existed in the same form in 2005. Some of the 1928 companies have ceased to exist.

Even though companies do change over time, we do not necessarily have to conclude that it is a mistake to organize our health-insurance system around employers. But it does provide a lot of food for thought.[9]

One problem with our current system is "job lock." Some employers provide health insurance, and others do not. As a result, some workers will decide to stay with their current job in order to maintain health-insurance coverage, even though another job might be better in other respects. Similarly, some people who are not working receive Medicaid benefits. Some of these people may decide not to get a job, if the job does not provide health insurance. However, if everyone is required to have health-insurance coverage, either through employment or through some other arrangement, job lock will be minimized.[10]

In this context, the health-insurance reform recently passed in Massachusetts is especially interesting. The new program in Massachusetts requires all

TABLE 4.2 Companies in the Dow Jones Industrial Average (DJIA), 1928 and 2005

DJIA COMPANIES AS OF OCTOBER 1, 1928	DJIA COMPANIES AS OF NOVEMBER 21, 2005
Allied Chemical	3M
American Can	Alcoa
American Smelting	Altria Group
American Sugar	American Express
American Tobacco	American International Group
Atlantic Refining	AT&T
Bethlehem Steel	Boeing
Chrysler	Caterpillar
General Electric	Citigroup
General Motors	Coca-Cola
General Railway Signal	DuPont
Goodrich	Exxon Mobil
International Harvester	General Electric
International Nickel	General Motors
Mack Truck	Hewlett-Packard
Nash Motors	Home Depot
North American	Honeywell International
Paramount Publix	Intel
Postum	International Business Machines
Radio Corporation	Johnson & Johnson
Sears Roebuck & Company	J. P. Morgan Chase
Standard Oil (New Jersey)	McDonald's
Texas Company	Merck
Texas Gulf Sulphur	Microsoft
Union Carbide	Pfizer
United States Steel	Procter & Gamble
Victor Talking Machine	United Technologies
Westinghouse Electric	Verizon
Woolworth	Wal-Mart Stores
Wright Aeronautical	Walt Disney

Source: http://djindexes.com/mdsidx/downloads/DJIA_Hist_Comp.pdf.

citizens to have medical insurance. Most Massachusetts residents would still get their insurance through their employers, but those who do not have employer-provided insurance would be required to obtain it from another source. Under the new program, most employers would have to pay additional fees if they do not provide insurance. The program also uses a carrot-and-stick approach to encourage uninsured individuals to get coverage: those with low incomes would receive subsidies, and those who do not acquire coverage would face penalties. Massachusetts would also expand eligibility for its Medicaid program. The plan's goal is for about 99.5 percent of the people of Massachusetts to have insurance within three years.

Critics of the Massachusetts program have raised two important objections. First, there is a concern over the budgetary cost to the Massachusetts government. According to the program's projections, most of the additional funding will come from federal sources. But of course it will make sense to keep careful track of the program's actual experience.

A second concern is that the stiffer requirements for employer-provided insurance will lead to a decrease in employment growth in Massachusetts. This raises a question: Is it best to make such changes at the state level, or at the national level? If fundamental health-insurance reform is to be undertaken, a case can be made for doing it nationally, rather than state by state. A nationwide reform would avoid any potential problem of penalizing the economy of an individual state that pursues medical-insurance reform on its own. For a further discussion of some of these issues, see Charles Ballard and John Goddeeris, "Financing Universal Health Care in the United States" (*National Tax Journal* 52 (1999): 31–52.

In some places in this book, I have made some very particular recommendations. In this section on health insurance, for better or worse, I have presented a menu of things to think about, without necessarily making strong recommendations. One reason for this is that the focus of this book is on *Michigan's* policies, but health insurance is an area in which *federal* policy is unusually important. If fundamental reform is to take place, it may well occur at the federal level. In that case, Michigan will have to adjust to whatever federal policies emerge.

In any case, Americans will have to face some difficult choices. As our population ages, and as more and more expensive medical technologies become available, spending pressures are expected to rise dramatically. It will be necessary for the private sector to come up with additional resources, or it will be necessary for state governments and the federal government to come up with additional resources, or we will have to ration access to health care by other means.

Michigan Policies Relating to Income Support

I emphasized education in chapter 2 because education is the surest path to a high-wage future. However, the payoff from education comes over a period of decades. We now turn our attention to some labor-market policies that have more of their effects in the short term. The first of these policies is the minimum wage, which has relatively small effects on government budgets. However, the minimum wage fits within the broader context of programs for low-wage workers. Many of these programs do have budgetary implications, and we will discuss some of them in this section.

The Minimum Wage

Currently, the federal minimum wage is $5.15 per hour. In March 2006, Michigan passed a law mandating a minimum wage above the federal minimum. The increase will be phased in over a two-year period. By July 2008, the minimum wage in Michigan will be $7.40 per hour.

Rebecca Blank of the University of Michigan discusses the minimum wage in *Michigan at the Millennium*. Minimum-wage laws have different effects on different groups of workers. For the vast majority of workers in Michigan (and in the rest of the United States), wage rates are well above the minimum wage. The minimum-wage law has no direct effect on these workers. The only workers who are affected directly by the minimum wage are those who face low wage rates. Fortunately, this is a relatively small group of workers.

Some low-wage workers will be helped by the increase in the minimum wage, because they will continue to work while receiving a higher wage rate. For a person working a 40-hour week for 50 weeks per year, the increase in the minimum wage from $5.15 to $7.40 would increase annual earnings from $10,300 to $14,800. That is an increase of $4,500 per year. If the affected worker is the head of a low-income household, this would make a tremendous difference.

However, this positive result will not occur if the worker is unable to find or keep a job. The minimum-wage law will harm some low-wage workers, because they will lose their jobs or they will be unable to find work in the first place. Consider a worker who is able to produce $6 per hour of value for his or her employer. If the minimum wage were at its current level of $5.15, or at any other level that is less than or equal to $6, this person would be employed and would earn $6 per hour. But when the minimum wage rises to $7.40, if employers obey the law, it may be very difficult for this worker to find and keep a job. As a result, instead of earning $6 per hour, this worker may earn zero.

This is one of the reasons why unemployment rates for teenagers are so much higher than unemployment rates for adults: teenagers are more likely to have the low levels of productivity that would merit a wage rate below the minimum wage. In the United States in 2005, the unemployment rate was 16.6 percent for workers aged 16–19, versus only 4.0 percent for workers aged 25–64.[11] Of course, the minimum wage is not the only reason for the difference between the unemployment rates of teenagers and adults, but minimum-wage laws probably explain a part of the difference.

There is an active debate in the economics profession about the size of the employment losses that will be brought on by an increase in the minimum wage. When the minimum wage goes up, how many workers will keep their jobs and earn more, and how many will be out of work? Charles Brown of the University of Michigan has written a thorough survey of the literature on the subject.[12] According to many of the studies surveyed by Brown, a 10 percent increase in the minimum wage would lead to a loss of youth employment of 1 percent or less.

Of course, the existing literature consists primarily of studies based on data sets in which the wage rates are substantially lower than $7.40 per hour. Therefore, in order to predict the effect of increasing Michigan's minimum wage to $7.40, it is necessary to make an extrapolation. Thus, we cannot be absolutely certain of the size of the employment losses that will occur. Nevertheless, it is useful to get a sense of the effect that might occur if the results from the existing literature turn out to be a reliable guide. The increase from $5.15 to $7.40 means that the minimum wage in Michigan will rise by more than 40 percent. Based on Brown's analysis of the literature, we might expect to see a loss of youth employment of something like 2 or 3 or 4 percent.

Thus, the good news is that the employment losses are likely to be relatively small. The bad news is that *any* increase in unemployment, especially among young people, would be an unfortunate side effect of the increase in the minimum wage. High youth unemployment can lead to a variety of long-term problems for society.

Supporters of the minimum wage often speak of it as an antipoverty measure. However, it should be noted that the minimum-wage law does not specifically target poor families. Many of the people who receive the minimum wage and are able to keep their jobs are teenagers in affluent families. Minimum-wage laws are not a terribly efficient method of fighting poverty, since young people in high-income households are among those who may reap benefits from an increase in the minimum wage, and some people in low-income households may be unable to find work.

The Earned Income Tax Credit

While I am hopeful that the increased minimum wage in Michigan will be beneficial to some low-wage workers, and that the employment losses will be relatively small, I also hope that we can redirect the debate toward policies other than the minimum wage. In fact, minimum-wage laws are not the only means by which we can fight poverty. An alternative is the Earned Income Tax Credit (EITC).[13] The federal EITC was instituted in 1975, during the presidency of Gerald Ford. The EITC was expanded in 1986 (under Ronald Reagan), in 1990 (under George H. W. Bush), and in 1993 (under Bill Clinton). Unlike the minimum wage, the EITC specifically targets low-income families. The EITC is an earnings subsidy for the workers with the lowest earnings in the labor market. Thus, while the minimum wage is likely to *reduce* employment, the EITC actually *increases* employment for certain groups of low-wage workers.

Seventeen states have chosen to augment the federal EITC, and the results are encouraging.[14] So far, Michigan is *not* one of the states that have increased the EITC. However, a Michigan EITC is well worth considering.

If the EITC has so many advantages over the minimum wage, why has the policy process in Michigan resulted in a higher minimum wage, rather than an EITC? One possibility is that the facts are not well understood. (Indeed, one of the purposes of this book is to get the word out on topics like this.) Another possibility has to do with the fact that the EITC has more direct implications for the government budget than does the minimum wage. For example, if Michigan were to adopt an EITC similar to the federal EITC, it would operate as a "refundable" tax credit: some people would see a reduction in their income-tax payments, and the government would send rebates to those whose income-tax payments were reduced to zero.[15] Since an EITC of this type would both reduce tax revenues and increase government expenditures, it presents a problem in a climate of chronic budgetary crises. However, that does not mean that the EITC is not a good policy.

Welfare Programs

Rebecca Blank discusses both the minimum wage and the EITC in *Michigan at the Millennium*. Blank also discusses a wide variety of other policies aimed at the low-wage labor market, including child-care and health-care programs. The effects of these policies for low-wage, low-skill workers are closely connected to the effects of welfare and public-assistance programs. "Welfare" programs provide cash support for low-income families, and sometimes for low-income individuals. These programs sometimes involve people who are not working. However, as we shall see, the trend is toward requiring benefit recipients to work. *Michigan at the Millennium* contains a thorough discussion of the welfare programs in Michigan by Kristin Seefeldt, Sheldon Danziger, and Sandra Danziger, all of the University of Michigan.

Until 1996, the main "welfare" program in the United States was the Aid to Families with Dependent Children program (AFDC). The federal government provided much of the funding for the program, but the individual states had considerable freedom to set their own benefit rules. In the 1970s, AFDC caseloads doubled in Michigan, reflecting a nationwide trend. Many of the changes since then can be seen as an extended reaction to the rapid growth of the program in the 1960s and 1970s. Seefeldt, Danziger, and Danziger devote much of their chapter to a discussion of the history of income-support programs, because the programs have changed repeatedly in the last 25 years or so. In 1981, a federal law made the eligibility requirements for welfare recipients more restrictive. A 1988 federal law put greater emphasis on education and training, but did not alter the basic structure of eligibility.

In the early 1990s, much of the impetus for changes to public-assistance programs came from state governments. A major change occurred in Michigan in 1991, when the General Assistance program was eliminated. General Assistance had provided benefits to low-income persons who were ineligible for AFDC or for federal disability programs. Some 80,000 individuals lost their benefits when the program was terminated. Michigan was also one of several states that obtained "waivers," whereby the federal government allowed the states to experiment with changes in the AFDC rules. Michigan's waivers involved changes in the benefit formula in an attempt to encourage program participants to work, as well as increased penalties for not participating in education or training activities. Also, monthly benefits in many states (including Michigan) were staying the same or falling. After adjusting for inflation, real benefit levels decreased.

The largest change of all came in August 1996, when President Clinton signed a new law fulfilling his pledge to "end welfare as we know it." This law, known by its acronym PRWORA,[16] replaced the federal entitlement to benefits with a set of block grants to the states. It continued the move in the direction of requiring participants to work in order to be eligible to receive benefits. Partly as a result of the work requirements, and partly as a result of the booming economy of the late 1990s, welfare caseloads dropped rapidly. The 2001 recession brought an increase in welfare caseloads in Michigan, but this increase was very small when compared with the huge decreases of earlier years. In October 1995, about 186,000 Michigan families were receiving benefits. By July 2002, the number was about 69,000.

The recovery from the 2001 recession was slow, especially in Michigan, but the recession itself was not very severe. It remains to be seen how the welfare system will perform if the economy experiences a deeper downturn.

Seefeldt, Danziger, and Danziger suggest some ways in which we could improve the economic situation of the welfare population:

- *Education* is extremely important. Lack of a high-school diploma is one of the most important difficulties faced by people at the bottom of the economic ladder. Over the long haul, the best policy is to reduce the number of high-school dropouts. For those who have already dropped out, training and diploma-equivalent programs may help.
- *Transportation* is one of the largest barriers to employment for many women. Improved public transportation could make a big difference for some.

- *Streamlined procedures for assessment and referral* would help to identify welfare recipients who have mental-health and/or substance-abuse problems. Those who suffer from these problems are unlikely to improve their long-term economic situations unless they get treatment.
- *Community service jobs* have fallen out of favor, but public-service employment can be a first step toward better long-term employment prospects for some workers.
- *Supported-work situations* can help to provide supervision for individuals who are having difficulty in making the transition to work.

Some of the suggestions mentioned above are in line with programs already in place. However, few would say that the existing programs are doing everything they could possibly do. If the existing programs were expanded, or if new programs were established, it would cost money. In these tight budgetary times, it seems unlikely that large amounts of additional funding will be forthcoming. Nevertheless, if programs are carefully targeted, it may be possible to generate a substantial benefit for modest cost.

Poverty in Michigan and in the Rest of the United States

So far in this section, we have discussed a number of laws and programs aimed (at least in part) at Michigan residents who are at or below the poverty line. In 2004, the official poverty line in the United States was in the neighborhood of $10,000 for a one-person household, $19,000 for a four-person household, and $33,000 for a household with eight people. The Census Bureau calculates that about 1.3 million Michigan residents fell below the poverty line in 2004, for a poverty rate of 13.3 percent. The rate for the United States as a whole was 12.7 percent.

Figure 4.2 shows some trends in the poverty rate. The figure shows Michigan and the United States, and it also shows Mississippi (which usually has one of the highest poverty rates in the country) and Connecticut (which usually has one of the lowest rates).[17] The poverty rate in Michigan has historically been fairly close to the U.S. average, although Michigan's poverty rate showed noticeable improvement during the boom years of the late 1990s.

The poverty rate in the United States fell sharply in the 1960s and early 1970s. Since then, the poverty rate has had its ups and downs, but the overall

FIGURE 4.2 Poverty Rates for Selected States and the U.S., 1981–2003

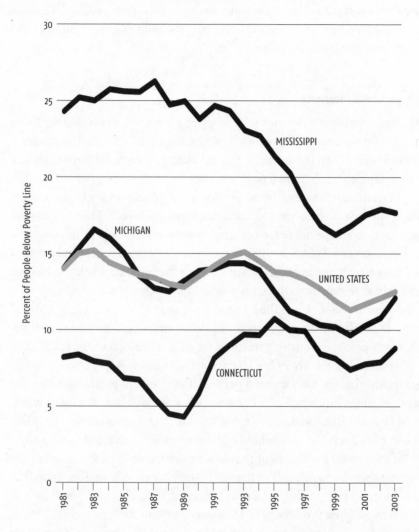

rate is actually higher today than in 1973. Clearly, our antipoverty programs have not been enough to overcome this disappointing trend. On the other hand, it does not make sense to expect antipoverty programs to turn the tide when so many forces are pushing in the opposite direction. As mentioned earlier in this book, the gap between high-income and low-income Americans has been widening for 30 years. And the biggest antipoverty program of all—the education system—has turned in a mediocre performance. Until we make major additional progress toward improving the skills of our population, the poverty rate is unlikely to drop very far.

Unemployment Insurance

The Unemployment Insurance (UI) program provides benefits that replace a portion of the earnings lost by workers who have been laid off. The program operates under federal guidelines, but the state governments have considerable freedom to set their own program rules.

UI benefits are financed by an employer payroll tax. In Michigan, the tax base is the first $9,000 paid to each employee each year. Thus, UI payroll taxes apply to a large portion of earnings for low-wage workers, but only to a small portion of earnings for high-wage workers. Sixteen states have indexed the UI tax base to the average level of wages in the state, but Michigan has not done this. Consequently, the UI tax base in Michigan has eroded very seriously over the years. When the UI system began in 1936, the tax base covered about 93 percent of the wages paid by taxable employers. By 2004 in Michigan, however, only about 20 percent of wages were subject to the tax.

The other key feature of the UI payroll tax is that it is "experience rated." This means that the tax rate for a particular employer is partly based on the employer's past history of layoffs: employers who have laid off a lot of workers will usually face a higher UI payroll tax rate than employers who have laid off fewer workers. The idea behind experience rating is to avoid forcing companies with stable employment to subsidize companies that lay off relatively large numbers of workers. The details of the tax-rate calculation, as well as other aspects of the Michigan UI program, are discussed in *Michigan at the Millennium* by Stephen Woodbury of Michigan State University.

The system of experience rating is not perfect. For example, there is no clear way to assign an experience rating to a new company, since new businesses do not have any history. In Michigan, all new employers are assigned a tax rate of 2.7 percent. For employers with a track record, there is a minimum tax rate, even for companies that have never laid anyone off. And there is a maximum tax rate, even for companies that engage in lots of layoffs. Thus, the system still subsidizes high-layoff employers and penalizes low-layoff employers (although the subsidies are smaller than they would be if experience rating were not used at all).

Because of the experience-rating system, high-layoff employers have an incentive to "dump" their tax liability. This is done by creating a new business entity (which will face the standard tax rate for new employers), and transferring workers to the new entity. The high-layoff employer still exists, but many of its workers have been shifted to a phony company for the purpose of evading UI taxes. This practice of "dumping" is a threat to the integrity of the UI system.

In 2005, the State of Michigan passed a new law to make it more difficult for employers to engage in dumping. This new law is a step in the right direction. In the future, it would be a good idea for the people of Michigan to monitor the effects of the antidumping law, and to consider other reforms of the UI system. These include refinements to the experience-rating system, as well as increases in the tax base. If the tax *base* were increased, the tax *rate* could be decreased.

For more thoughts on UI, as well as on worker's compensation and worker-training programs, see the *Michigan at the Millennium* chapter by Stephen Woodbury.

Conclusion

In earlier chapters, we have taken a look at some programs that have important implications for government budgets in Michigan. In this chapter, we began by considering the overall budget of the State of Michigan. We then moved on to consider some other specific programs that have important effects on the budget, including corrections, health care, and programs for low-wage, low-income, and unemployed residents.

The most important idea in this chapter is that the budget of the State of Michigan faces chronic *structural* deficits. The cost of maintaining programs is increasing relative to tax revenues, even in good economic times. By itself, robust economic growth will *not* be enough to change the situation. Of course, a higher rate of economic growth is better for the budget than a lower rate of economic growth. But the people of Michigan will be deluding themselves if they think that economic growth alone will solve the long-run budgetary problems. Instead, it will be necessary to make choices. The choices will not be easy, but they cannot be avoided either.

In part, the structural deficits arise because of problems with the tax system. Every major source of tax revenue in Michigan has structural problems. (For example, the sales tax applies to very few services. Since services are growing faster than the overall economy, the nontaxation of services means that sales-tax revenues do not keep up.) As a result of these structural problems, tax revenue grows more slowly than the Michigan economy, even when tax rates remain the same. The tax cuts of recent years have added to the trend of shrinking tax revenues. However, the structural problems of the tax system are such that tax revenues would bring in a decreasing percentage of personal income, even if tax rates had been unchanged.

The tax system will be discussed in much more detail in chapter 5. The rest of this chapter was devoted to looking at categories of government expenditure in Michigan. Here are some of the highlights:

- Gross expenditures by the State of Michigan are dominated by a small number of categories. In particular, well over half of these expenditures are for school aid and community health. However, not all of the gross expenditures are actually financed by Michigan taxpayers; a substantial portion comes from the federal government, especially in the Medicaid program.
- The fastest growing category of expenditure is corrections. From 1982 to 2002, the number of prisoners under the jurisdiction of the State of Michigan increased from about 13,000 to about 49,000. The incarceration rate is substantially higher in Michigan than in neighboring states. This is partly due to the use of longer prison sentences in Michigan. If the incarceration rate were the same in Michigan as in the other states in the Great Lakes region, prison expenditures in Michigan would be reduced by about $500 million per year.
- Community health is second only to school aid in terms of its effect on the Michigan budget. If we were to construct a single category including all health-related expenditures (such as health care for prisoners, and health care for current and retired government employees), it would be the largest category of all.
- Health-care spending has grown tremendously in the last several decades, and it is expected to continue to grow much more rapidly than the rest of

the economy. This is partly because of the aging of the population, and partly because it is expected that expensive new medical techniques will continue to be developed. There is every indication that health-care spending (and Medicaid spending in particular) will continue to exert great pressure on the Michigan budget. It will either be necessary to increase revenues, or to reduce health-care expenditures, or to reduce spending on other programs. None of these options will be easy.

- In 2004, nearly 89 percent of Michigan residents had some form of health insurance. Fortunately, this is well above the national average. Unfortunately, it still means that more than a million people in Michigan are without insurance coverage. Massachusetts recently passed a law that is projected to achieve insurance coverage in excess of 99 percent of the population. It will be interesting to observe the progress of the Massachusetts plan.

- Michigan recently passed a law that will raise the minimum wage by more than 40 percent by 2008. Some low-wage workers will be able to earn more as a result. However, others may lose their jobs, or may find it impossible to get a job in the first place. Fortunately, the economic literature suggests that the job losses will be relatively small, but any losses of employment would be an adverse side effect of the law. Another problem with the minimum wage is that it is not targeted toward low-income families. Some of the affected workers are teenagers in affluent families.

- Seventeen states have augmented the federal Earned Income Tax Credit (EITC), but Michigan is not one of them. Nevertheless, because of the drawbacks of the minimum wage, an EITC is a policy option to consider for the future. The EITC is an earnings subsidy, and it will tend to increase employment. In addition, the EITC can be targeted toward low-income families.

- The number of people receiving public-assistance payments grew dramatically in the 1970s. Since then, a series of changes in state law and federal law have reduced the generosity of these programs. In Michigan, the General Assistance program was eliminated in 1991. The federal welfare-reform law of 1996 continued a trend toward requiring participants to work in order to be eligible for benefits. From 1995 to 2002, there was a decrease of almost two-thirds in the number of Michigan families receiving welfare payments.

Improved education and training have the greatest potential to help the population of low-skill workers who have traditionally been served by welfare programs. Transportation, assessment and referral for mental-health and substance-abuse programs, and supported-work situations could also improve the lives of people in low-income households.

- The payroll tax for Unemployment Insurance (UI) only applies to the first $9,000 paid to each employee each year. This means that the tax base applies to a large portion of earnings for low-wage workers, and a small portion of earnings for high-wage workers. If the tax base were increased, it would be possible to raise the same amount of tax revenue with a lower tax rate.

- The UI payroll tax is "experience rated," which means that the tax rate is higher for businesses that have laid off a lot of workers. However, the system of experience rating is incomplete, and this means that high-layoff employers are still subsidized by low-layoff employers. Further strengthening of experience rating has the potential to improve both the efficiency and the fairness of the UI system.

Some employers have engaged in "dumping" of their UI tax liability by transferring workers to new companies that have been created for the purpose of evading UI taxes. The State of Michigan recently passed a law designed to limit this practice. The progress of the system should be monitored, to make sure that the law is having the intended effect.

NOTES

1. These data are taken from the website of the Office of the State Budget, at *http://www.michigan.gov/documents/Agency_Budget_schedules_58910_7.pdf*.

2. Gary Olson provides a detailed discussion of the constitutional and statutory rules governing the budget of the State of Michigan in *Michigan at the Millennium*.

3. Thomas Clay of the Citizens Research Council of Michigan provides an excellent discussion of the structural deficit and related issues, in "Michigan's Budget Crisis and the Prospects for the Future," available at *http://www.crcmich.org*.

4. The nominal expenditure data are taken from Gary Olson's chapter in *Michigan at the Millennium*. The inflation adjustment is based on data from the website of the U.S. Commerce Department's Bureau of Economic Analysis, at *http://www.bea.gov/bea/dn/nipaweb/index.asp*.

5. See "Michigan's Budget Crisis and the Prospects for the Future," by Thomas Clay, at http://www.crcmich.org.

6. The increase in the cigarette tax is certain to improve some aspects of the health of Michigan's people. The long-term effects on the budget are less clear. In the near term, the higher tax on cigarettes will bring in more revenues for the state government. However, over a period of many years, cigarette-tax revenues may decline if there is a sufficiently large decrease in the number of smokers. Also, if people stop smoking, they will live longer. There may be a reduction in lung cancer, heart disease, and other tobacco-related illnesses, but those who live longer may eventually suffer from other diseases. These other diseases will have an effect on health-care spending. For me, however, this is not a very important consideration. I would much rather have people live, and deal with their old-age health problems when the time comes, rather than allow them to go to an early death from smoking.

7. These data are from Carmen DeNavas-Walt, Bernadette Proctor, and Cheryl Hill Lee, U.S. Census Bureau, Current Population Reports, P60-229, "Income, Poverty, and Health Insurance Coverage in the United States: 2004," available at http://www.census.gov/prod/2005pubs/p60-229.pdf.

8. These projections are available at http://www.gpoaccess.gov/usbudget/fy07/sheets/hist11z3.xls.

9. For the same reason, a strong case can also be made for avoiding defined-benefit pension plans that are tied to the financial well-being of a particular company. Defined-contribution pension plans are also a problem if asset portfolios are not diversified, as many former Enron employees learned painfully.

10. Another advantage of a mandatory system has to do with the tax subsidy for employer-provided health insurance. Currently, governments in the United States provide a huge subsidy to employers in an attempt to encourage them to provide health insurance. The subsidy operates through the tax system: whereas wages and salaries are subject to the income tax and the payroll tax, employer-provided health insurance is excluded from the income-tax base and the payroll-tax base. The revenue loss to the federal government alone is about $180 billion per year, and that does not even include the revenue losses for state governments. If a system of mandatory insurance coverage were instituted, these subsidies could be reduced or eliminated, and the money could be used for a variety of other purposes.

11. These data are taken from the website of the Bureau of Labor Statistics, at http://stats.bls.gov/cps/cpsaat3.pdf.

12. See Charles Brown, "Minimum Wages, Employment, and the Distribution of Income," in Orley Ashenfelter and David Card, eds., Handbook of Labor Economics, vol. 3B (Amsterdam: Elsevier North Holland, 1999).

13. The EITC is another policy discussed in the *Michigan at the Millennium* chapter by the University of Michigan's Rebecca Blank. For further discussion of the EITC, see Joseph Hotz and Karl Scholz, "Not Perfect But Still Pretty Good: The EITC and Other Policies to Support the U.S. Low-Wage Labor Market" (*OECD Economic Studies* 31 (2000): 26–42.

14. See Scott Darragh, "The Impact of the Earned Income Tax Credit on Poverty, Labor Supply, and Human-Capital Accumulation," Ph.D. diss., Michigan State University, 2002.

15. Michigan's Homestead Property Tax Credit is another example of a refundable credit.

16. PRWORA stands for Personal Responsibility and Work Opportunity Reconciliation Act.

17. The data for figure 4.2 are taken from the Census Bureau website, "Historical Poverty Tables, Table 21, Number of Poor and Poverty Rate, by State: 1980 to 2004," available at *http://www.census.gov/hhes/www/poverty/histpov/hstpov21.html*. The data for individual states can fluctuate by a fairly large amount because of small sample sizes. Therefore, for the three states shown, we use a three-year average.

The Tax System in Michigan

In the words of Supreme Court Justice Oliver Wendell Holmes Jr., "Taxes are what we pay for civilized society." On the other hand, nobody enjoys paying taxes, and taxes can damage the workings of the economy. The tension between the benefits of public services and the costs imposed by taxes is at the heart of some of the most important concerns of public economics.

One of the central objectives of tax policy is to choose the *best possible overall level* of taxes. Another objective is to choose the *best possible mix* of income taxes, sales taxes, property taxes, and other revenue sources. These two issues are closely related, and I will discuss both of them in this chapter. I will argue for changes in the overall level of taxes, and I will also argue for changes in the mix of taxes in Michigan.

First, however, let us begin with a brief tour of the tax system in Michigan. When I discuss the tax system, I will usually focus on the *combined* tax systems of the state government and the various local governments. In Michigan (as in most states), local governments and school districts receive a great deal of their funding from the state government. Therefore, it usually makes sense to think of the state tax system and the local tax systems as parts of a whole, rather than as separate entities.

A Brief Overview of the Michigan Tax System

In many ways, the Michigan tax system is similar to the state and local tax systems in most states. Michigan has an individual income tax, as do 42 other states and the District of Columbia.[1] Michigan also has a general retail sales tax, as do 45 other states and the District of Columbia.[2] Every one of the 50 states and D.C. uses property taxes (which are especially important for local governments), as well as taxes on alcoholic beverages, tobacco products, and motor fuels. For more details on the overall structure of the tax system in Michigan, see my chapter, "Overview of Michigan's Revenue System," in *Michigan at the Millennium*.

Table 5.1 compares the state and local tax system in Michigan with the average of the state and local tax systems in the United States, for 2003–2004.[3] The table shows that the percentage composition of Michigan's state and local tax system is fairly similar to the average composition of the state and local tax systems in the United States as a whole. Property taxes account for about 35.8 percent of tax revenues in Michigan, versus about 31.5 percent of state and local tax revenues nationwide. The general retail sales tax provides about 23.6 percent of the tax revenues in Michigan, and about 24.2 percent of the state and local taxes in the United States overall. Individual income taxes account for about 19 percent of the tax revenues in Michigan, and about 21.3 percent for the nation as a whole. Thus, if we add together the three main pillars of the state and local tax system (property taxes, general sales taxes, and individual income taxes), we have about 78 percent of tax revenues in Michigan, and about 77 percent of state and local tax revenues nationally.

However, there are some notable differences between the tax system in Michigan and the systems in other states. As seen in table 5.1, tobacco taxes account for a much larger percentage of tax revenues in Michigan.[4] The tax system in Michigan also relies relatively heavily on motor-vehicle license taxes. In the next few paragraphs, we will discuss some other unusual aspects of the Michigan tax system.

The Centralization of the Tax System in Michigan

The state and local tax system is more dominated by *state* taxes in Michigan than in most states. In 2003–2004, about 67.6 percent of the state and local

TABLE 5.1 Revenues for Selected Taxes, as Percentage of Total Tax Revenues, for Michigan and the United States, 2003–2004

	AS PERCENT OF STATE AND LOCAL TAXES	
TAX	IN MICHIGAN	IN THE UNITED STATES
Property Taxes	35.78	31.50
General Retail Sales Taxes	23.58	24.24
Individual Income Taxes	19.00	21.30
Motor Fuel Taxes	3.23	3.46
Motor Vehicle License Taxes	3.19	1.85
Tobacco Taxes	2.98	1.25

Source: Author's calculations based on U.S. Census Bureau, State and Local Government Finances: 2003–2004. Available at http://www.census.gov/govs/www/estimate04.html.

Note: The column totals do not add to 100 percent, because some small categories of taxes have not been included.

taxes in Michigan were collected by the state government. This compares with about 58.4 percent for the nation as a whole. Michigan did not always have such a centralized tax system. However, as a result of the passage of Proposal A in 1994, local property taxes were reduced substantially. Proposal A replaced a portion of the lost revenue with increases in the sales tax and the cigarette tax, both of which are levied by the state government. Proposal A also introduced a new property tax at the state level, known as the "State Education Tax."[5] Consequently, control over revenues is heavily concentrated at the state level, so that local governments and public schools have less control over their finances in Michigan than in most other states.

Michigan's Flat-Rate Income Tax

Michigan is one of only six states in which the individual income tax has only a single rate.[6] (Currently, the tax rate on all taxable income in Michigan is 3.9 percent.) By contrast, the individual income taxes in most other states, as well as the federal individual income tax, have "graduated marginal tax rates." When an income tax has graduated rates, the tax rate on an additional dollar of income is higher for those with larger incomes. For example, in California, the tax rate on the first dollar of taxable income is 1 percent. However, California's income tax has six marginal tax rates. The highest of these is 9.3 percent, which takes effect when a married couple has taxable income of slightly more than $80,000. Thus, when compared to a graduated income tax that raises the same amount of revenue, Michigan's income tax collects relatively more from low-income residents, and relatively less from those with high incomes.[7]

The Single Business Tax

Michigan had a corporate income tax in the late 1960s and early 1970s, but replaced it with the Single Business Tax (SBT) in 1975. The SBT also replaced six other taxes on businesses—hence the name "Single" Business Tax.

James Hines of the University of Michigan discusses the SBT in detail in *Michigan at the Millennium*. The tax base for the SBT consists mainly of the profits of the business, plus employee compensation, depreciation, and interest paid. Forty-five of the 50 states still have a corporate income tax, but no other state has adopted a tax like the SBT.[8] We will discuss the SBT in much greater detail later in this chapter.

The Level of Taxes

Figure 5.1 shows some of the trends in the percentage of personal income that goes to state and local taxes. The figure covers the years from 1972 to 2004.[9] Figure 5.1 shows the trends for Michigan and the United States as a whole, as well as for New York (because its taxes are persistently among the highest in the country) and Texas (because its taxes are persistently among the lowest).

Perhaps the most important trend shown in figure 5.1 is the significant decrease in the percentage of income that goes to state and local taxes. For the United States as a whole, state and local taxes dropped from about 12.8 percent of income in 1972 to about 11 percent in 2004. Michigan's state and local taxes have been fairly close to the U.S. average for most of the last 30 years, especially when viewed against the background of the taxes in states like New York and Texas. However, the decrease in state and local taxes has been even sharper in Michigan than in the rest of the country. In Michigan, state and

FIGURE 5.1 State and Local Taxes as Percent of Personal Income, 1972–2004

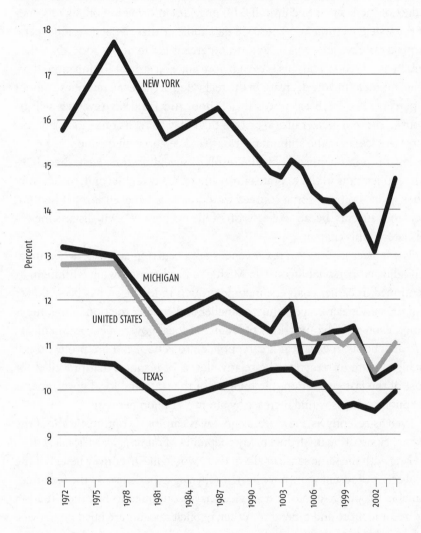

local taxes fell from about 13.2 percent of income in 1972 to about 10.5 percent of income in 2004. As a result of this substantial decline, taxes in Michigan fell from slightly above the national average in the 1970s and 1980s to slightly below the national average by 2004.

Figure 5.1 shows information for state and local governments combined. If we consider the state government by itself, tax revenues have been especially weak in recent years. For example, the Department of Management and Budget of the State of Michigan (DMB) provides information on tax revenues for the state government.[10] The DMB data indicate that General Fund/General Purpose tax revenues will be about 1.6 percent *less* in 2005–2006 than they were in 2002–2003, and this is even before any adjustment for inflation. If we adjust for inflation, the decrease in the real value of these tax revenues is about 10 percent. The DMB calculates that School Aid Fund tax revenues will be about 5.1 percent greater in 2005–2006 than they were in 2002–2003, but this increase is less than the amount necessary to keep up with inflation.

The drop in tax revenues is the result of several factors. First, there have been explicit cuts in the tax rates for some of the taxes. Second, the tax revenues collected from some sources would have fallen even if there had not been any rate cuts, because of erosion of the tax base. We will discuss the details later in this chapter.

These steep declines in tax revenues are occurring at a time when inflation-adjusted personal income in Michigan has been growing (although, as mentioned in earlier chapters, income growth in Michigan has been slower than the national average). Thus, a smaller and smaller fraction of income is being devoted to the functions of state and local government in Michigan, such as schools, roads, health care, police protection, and fire protection. If Michigan were to return to the relative levels of taxation that prevailed for most of the last generation, the budgets of the state and local governments and public schools would increase by about $5 billion per year.

Even as recently as a few years ago, I was cautiously optimistic about the budgetary situation in Michigan. My chapter in *Michigan at the Millennium* does not ring with the same sense of alarm that I would like to convey here. But the fiscal crises of recent years have been a sobering experience. As the resources available for public goods and services have continued to fall, the situation has become more and more dire. When explicit tax cuts are piled on top of a badly eroded tax base, the result is a tax system that is increasingly out of step with the revenue needs of today and tomorrow.

Unless the trend is reversed, it will be more and more difficult for Michigan to provide the education system and other public services that its citizens deserve. Of course, it is *always* good policy to examine and reexamine the expenditures of government, in search of savings. However, the fiscal crises of recent years have already caused a tremendous amount of belt tightening in the state and local government budgets in Michigan (except in corrections). Although further economizing must be a *part* of the solution, it cannot be the *entire* solution. If we could provide the public services that are essential for Michigan's future without at least some increases in taxes, I would be the first to say so. In my view, however, it just is not possible.

I certainly understand that a call for more public revenues is controversial. But I want to make clear that I am not suggesting a radical increase in taxes in Michigan. Instead, I am suggesting a fairly modest reversal of the trends of recent years. The percentage of income that is paid in taxes in Michigan is lower now than it has been in decades. We could have a substantial *increase* in tax revenues and still be *below* the tax levels of 30 years ago. Thus, I am not calling for tax increases that would take us into uncharted waters. Instead, I am calling for a return to levels of taxation under which the people of Michigan have prospered in the past.

In my view, the main obstacles to improving the tax system in Michigan are political, rather than economic. In an earlier chapter of this book, I related a conversation with a student who suggested it would be "political suicide" to raise taxes. As I said then, if it is political suicide to do what needs to be done for the future of Michigan's economy, then we're dead already.

In the next few pages, I will discuss some specific aspects of the Michigan tax system that have contributed to the decline in tax revenues. Throughout this chapter, the discussion will be framed in terms of the need to collect an adequate amount of revenue. However, it makes no sense to flail about wildly in search of tax revenues. The search must be focused. Thus, some of the tax reforms discussed in this chapter do not involve additional revenues at all. And when a suggested reform does raise additional revenues, the reform is recommended because it would also advance other goals, such as improving the efficiency or fairness of Michigan's tax system.

Termites in the Tax Base

In some cases, tax revenues can go down as a result of deliberate changes in tax policy. Indeed, policy changes in Michigan have led to revenue reductions on several occasions in the last decade or so. In 1994, Proposal A involved some tax-rate increases, as well as some rate cuts, but the net effect was a decrease in tax revenues. Then, beginning in 1999, the marginal tax rate in the individual income tax was reduced repeatedly, as was the tax rate in the Single Business Tax. [11]

However, tax revenues can also change, even when there is no explicit change in tax policy. For example, when the economy stalled in 2000 and slipped into recession in 2001, tax revenues in Michigan would have fallen even if there had not been any changes in the tax laws. The downward slide of revenues was exacerbated by the cuts in tax rates.

Now, however, the recession of 2001 is long gone, and yet tax revenues continue to grow sluggishly. Clearly, the business cycle is not the only influence on tax revenues. In fact, the tax system in Michigan has serious structural weaknesses. These weaknesses cause tax revenues to decline year after year—even when the economy is not sinking, and even when there are no tax-rate cuts. There are structural weaknesses in the sales tax, the income tax, and the taxes on beer, wine, tobacco, and motor fuels, and I will discuss each of them in this section. The property tax also suffers from structural weaknesses. (I will discuss the property tax later in this chapter.) Most of the revenue reductions of recent years are due to structural problems, rather than to explicit cuts in tax rates.

Erosion of the Sales-Tax Base

Joel Slemrod of the University of Michigan provides a detailed discussion of the general retail sales tax in *Michigan at the Millennium*. One of the most important features of the sales tax in most states, including Michigan, is that most services are exempt. Michigan's sales tax does not apply to accounting services, beauty parlors, car washes, carpentry services, dance lessons, dating services, health clubs, laundry and dry-cleaning services, lawn-care services, legal services, movie-theater admissions, pet-grooming services, plumbing services, real-estate-agent services, tanning parlors, tax-return preparation services, veterinary services, and a host of other services.

The Federation of Tax Administrators has published information on the taxation of services in 2004, available at *http://www.taxadmin.org/fta/pub/ services/services.html*. This report lists 168 service categories. Only Hawaii and New Mexico come close to comprehensive taxation of services. The median state taxes 55 categories. Michigan taxes only 26 of the 168 categories. (Some

38 states and the District of Columbia tax more categories of services than are taxed in Michigan.)

Several of the services that *are* taxed in Michigan are business services. As pointed out in Slemrod's chapter in *Michigan at the Millennium,* an efficient tax system would *not* involve taxes on business-to-business sales. Thus, Michigan's sales tax manages to tax some things that should not be taxed, while failing to tax a large number of items that could be taxed in such a way as to enhance the efficiency of the tax system.

At one time, the nontaxation of services did not make a huge difference, because services were a relatively small part of the economy. But services have grown more rapidly than the rest of the economy for the last couple of generations. As we saw in chapter 1 of this book, services are now the biggest single part of the economy.

Thus, the revenue losses from nontaxation of services are very large, and they grow larger every year. The Michigan Department of Treasury has estimated the size of the revenue losses in the "Executive Budget: Tax Expenditure Appendix, Fiscal Year 2004."[12] (A "tax expenditure" is the number of dollars by which potential tax revenues are decreased as a result of some provision of the tax code. The estimates are not perfect, because they assume that taxpayers do not change their behavior in response to changes in taxation. However, the estimates are probably a good approximation.)

The Tax Expenditure Appendix lists dozens of holes in the Michigan tax system, totaling about $27 billion of annual revenue losses. By far the largest of these is the nontaxation of services in the sales tax, which is estimated to have accounted for about $7.3 billion of lost tax revenues in 2004. This annual revenue loss from not taxing services is almost as large as the amount collected by the sales tax. This points the way toward reform of the tax system. Instead of taxing some things at 6 percent, and taxing services at zero percent, we could bring more services into the tax base and raise the same amount of revenue with a tax rate substantially lower than 6 percent.[13] This has the potential to raise the same number of dollars that we raise now, in a much more efficient manner.[14] In light of the ongoing budgetary crisis, an even more attractive policy would be the following: If the sales tax were extended to a broader range of services, it would be possible to raise *additional* revenue while still *reducing* the sales-tax rate on the things that are taxed.

In response to proposals to expand the sales tax to cover more services, one sometimes hears the following objection: If we tax a sector of the economy that has previously been untaxed, there will be employment losses in that sector. That may be true (although those who raise the objection have an incentive to overstate the problem in an attempt to maintain political support for their privileged treatment). However, it is important to keep this in perspective. If tanning parlors have been untaxed in the past while other things have been taxed, tanning parlors may well have grown more rapidly than they would otherwise have grown. (It is not surprising that activities tend to grow faster when they receive preferential treatment.) Thus, if the privileged tax treatment of tanning parlors were removed, the tanning-parlor sector would probably grow less rapidly, and there could be some employment losses there.

However, the situation would be reversed in the sectors of the economy that were previously penalized. Just as the untaxed services have benefited from the unlevel playing field, the taxed activities have been penalized by it. If the playing field were leveled, there might be job losses in the sectors that have previously been privileged, but there would also be job gains in the sectors that have previously been punished. There is no reason to believe that the *overall* level of employment would be harmed substantially. In fact, overall employment might increase, because the reformed tax system would allow for a more efficient allocation of resources in the economy.[15]

It will not be easy to reform the sales tax in Michigan. Lobbyists will fight hard to maintain the privileged status of each of the services that currently gets preferential treatment. Nevertheless, if we continue with the current system, which taxes some activities at 6 percent while other activities get special treatment, the long-term effect will be the continued erosion of the tax base. This will perpetuate economic inefficiency, and it will damage our ability to pay for public services in Michigan.

If the states could coordinate their sales-tax policies, it would make for a better tax system nationwide. Michigan is involved in the Streamlined Sales Tax Project (SSTP), which aims to assist the states in administering a simpler and more uniform sales-tax system. For more information on the SSTP, see *http://www.streamlinedsalestax.org*.

Food purchased for home consumption is also not covered by the Michigan sales tax. This also creates a loss of tax revenue, although the revenue loss from nontaxation of food is smaller than the loss from nontaxation of services. The policy of not taxing food is usually justified in terms of its effect on the distribution of income, since the percentage of income spent on food is highest for low-income people. That is a valid concern. However, the exemption of food from the sales tax is a fairly blunt instrument for helping those with low incomes. After all, middle- and upper-income people also eat food. In fact, as we move up the income scale, the decrease in the percentage of income devoted to food is surprisingly slow. Higher-income people do not necessarily eat *more* food, but they do eat more expensive foods. Of course, it might be possible to tax food items that are consumed mainly by high-income folks, but that would open up the sales tax to endless wrangling. Where do we draw the line? Do we tax sirloin, but not roast beef? An alternative would be to tax food, and to offset the effect on low-income people by using a refundable credit in the income tax.

Erosion of the Income Tax Base

Paul Menchik of Michigan State University discusses the individual income tax in *Michigan at the Millennium*. In the Michigan individual income tax, the calculation of taxable income begins with adjusted gross income, which is taken directly from the federal tax return. This procedure simplifies the calculation of Michigan income-tax liability, and therefore reduces the taxpayer's cost of complying with the tax laws. However, it also means that many types of income are excluded from the tax base of the Michigan income tax because they have already been excluded from the federal tax base. (The largest items excluded from the tax base are the employer contributions for health insurance and pensions.)

The Michigan income tax also includes a personal exemption, which was $3,200 per person in 2005.[16] Additional exemptions are given for senior citizens, individuals with certain disabilities, and children under age 18. Senior citizens are also allowed to deduct Social Security benefits, dividends, interest, capital gains, and pension benefits. After these and a few other adjustments, the taxpayer calculates his or her taxable income. Taxable income is then multiplied by the flat tax rate, which is currently 3.9 percent. After that, taxpayers may further reduce their tax liabilities if they are able to claim certain tax credits. By far the largest of the tax credits is the Homestead Property Tax Credit, which effectively reduces property-tax liabilities. The Homestead Credit is larger for senior citizens than for the rest of the population.

Because of the various exclusions, deductions, exemptions, and credits, the revenue-raising capacity of the individual income tax is much smaller than it would otherwise be. If the tax base were less eroded, it would be possible to raise more revenue with the same tax rate, or to raise the same amount of revenue with a lower tax rate.

We have seen that senior citizens in Michigan receive a large number of special tax treatments. Seniors receive additional exemptions, and they are able to deduct large amounts of retirement income. Moreover, senior citizens receive extra Homestead credits. Senior citizens receive far more generous treatment from the Michigan income tax than from the income taxes in most other states. As emphasized by Paul Menchik in *Michigan at the Millennium*, the vast majority of senior citizens pay no income tax in Michigan. In fact, the total net amount of income tax paid by Michigan seniors is *negative*. (In other words, their refunds from the Homestead Property Tax Credit are larger than their tax payments.)

As discussed in chapter 2, Michigan's population is growing older. We can expect an increase in the proportion of the Michigan population who are senior citizens. Therefore, unless the extraordinary generosity of the tax system toward senior citizens is reduced, the revenue-raising capacity of the income tax will continue to shrink.

It is important to address one potential objection to reducing the generosity of the Michigan income tax toward senior citizens. Many elderly people have modest incomes, and it is very reasonable to ask whether these folks should have to pay more taxes. However, it should be remembered that the income tax already addresses this issue through the personal exemption. The purpose of the personal exemption is to shield low-income residents (young and old) from having to pay much income tax. Thus, the low-income elderly have never paid much income tax, and they still would not pay much income tax if some of the special tax treatments discussed here were removed. Most of the additional taxes would be paid by the affluent elderly.

The interests of the low-income elderly (as well as other low-income people) have *not* been a major consideration in Michigan tax policy in recent years. However, if there is a genuine desire to help the low-income elderly, there are ways to do it without exempting certain categories of income from taxation. For example, we could increase the personal exemption. Most of the benefits of the special provisions go to elderly residents who are not poor, whereas an increase in the personal exemption would benefit all low-income people (and not just the low-income elderly).

I am not under any illusions about the political obstacles to reducing the tax breaks for elderly Michigan residents. Politically, it will not be any easier to reform the income-tax treatment of senior citizens than to tax services, or to reform any other part of the tax system. Nevertheless, if we fail to bring the taxation of seniors more into line with the taxation of the rest of the population, the long-term effect will be the continued erosion of the tax base. This, in turn, will compromise our ability to deal with Michigan's fiscal challenges.

In recent pages, I have emphasized that it has become more difficult to raise revenue because of the erosion of the sales-tax base and the income-tax base. But shrinking revenues are not the only result of the nontaxation of services in the sales tax, and the generous tax treatment of senior citizens in the income tax. These tax policies also contradict basic principles of tax fairness.

The Peculiar Taxes on Beer, Wine, Tobacco, and Motor Fuels

All 50 states have taxes on beer, wine, tobacco products, and motor fuels. Lawrence Martin of Michigan State University discusses Michigan's taxes on alcohol and tobacco in *Michigan at the Millennium*. Kenneth Boyer, also of Michigan State University, discusses the motor-fuels taxes in the volume.

It is important to understand a fundamental difference between these taxes and most other taxes. Income taxes are levied as a *percentage* of taxable income. Property taxes are levied as a *percentage* of the assessed value of the property. Sales taxes are levied as a *percentage* of the price of the item. But most of the taxes on beer, wine, tobacco products, and motor fuels are different. Instead of being levied as a percentage of some dollar value, these taxes are "unit taxes." For example, the tax rates are expressed as a number of cents per gallon of gasoline, or a number of dollars per pack of cigarettes.

For the taxes that are expressed as a percentage of value, an increase in the price of the item leads automatically to an increase in the amount of tax per unit. However, for the "unit taxes," the amount of tax per unit is the same, regardless of the price. This creates two distinct problems. First, when inflation pushes prices higher and higher, the unit tax becomes a smaller and smaller percentage of the total price. Thus, the real revenue-raising capacity of these taxes is eroded over time, unless the legislature increases the tax rate explicitly.

In the case of cigarette taxes, this effect has been offset by legislated increases in the tax rate.[17] However, the unit tax on wine has been unchanged since 1981, and the unit tax on beer has stayed the same since 1962. In the four-plus decades since 1962, the overall price level has increased by more than 420 percent.[18] As a result, inflation has reduced the effective tax rates substantially, and this has seriously eroded the real revenue-raising capacity of these taxes. Also, the taxes on beer and wine are probably motivated by a desire to discourage the antisocial behaviors associated with excessive drinking. As the effective tax rate is reduced over time, the disincentive for binge drinking is also reduced.[19]

The second problem with unit taxes is that they create a strange kind of inequity. The cigarette tax in Michigan is $2 per pack. If a smoker buys a pack of cigarettes for $4, the Michigan tax is one-half of the price. On the other hand, if another smoker buys a pack of a premium brand of cigarettes for $6, the Michigan tax is only one-third of the price. Thus, the buyer of premium cigarettes pays a lower effective tax rate than the buyer of discount cigarettes. The same thing happens when people buy wine, beer, or gasoline: the folks who buy high-priced wines face a lower effective tax rate than those who buy the cheaper varieties, and the folks who buy premium gasoline face a lower effective tax rate than those who buy regular.

There is a clear-cut solution to these problems. We should replace the unit taxes with taxes levied as a percentage of sales price. In that way, inflation would no longer erode the revenues from these taxes over time. And the person who buys regular gasoline will not pay a higher effective tax rate than the one who buys premium. In the case of the cigarette tax, I am in favor of using the percentage tax rate that would raise the same amount of tax revenue as the current unit tax. For the taxes on beer and wine, a strong case can be made for using a percentage tax rate that would raise *more* revenue than is currently raised, to offset some of the erosion of the last few decades.

The taxes on motor fuels are also levied on a per-unit basis. In addition, Michigan is unusual in that the tax rate on diesel fuel is less than the tax rate on gasoline. In 2005, 27 states and the District of Columbia imposed the same tax on diesel fuel and gasoline, and 14 states and the federal government imposed a higher tax on diesel. Among the nine states with a lower tax on diesel fuel, the difference between the gasoline tax rate and the diesel-fuel tax rate was greatest in Michigan. Only five states had a lower excise tax on diesel fuel than Michigan.[20] Higher taxes on motor fuels would raise additional revenue, and they may also have environmental advantages. A strong case can be made for (1) raising the tax rates on both gasoline and diesel fuel, (2) raising the diesel tax rate more than the gasoline tax rate, and (3) converting both to a percentage basis.

The Effects of the Michigan Tax System on Different Income Classes

In the case of a "proportional" tax, people with different incomes pay the same percentage of their incomes in tax. If a tax is "progressive," an increase in income leads to an *increase* in the percentage paid in tax. If a tax is "regressive," a movement up the income scale leads to a *decrease* in the percentage paid in tax. Thus, a progressive tax takes relatively more from the people with the highest incomes, while a regressive tax takes relatively more from those with the lowest incomes.

As we have seen, the tax system in Michigan has a large number of distinct components. Some of these are progressive, while others are regressive. For further discussion of the effects of these taxes on the distribution of income, see my chapter in *Michigan at the Millennium*. A brief summary is provided here.

The Distributional Effects of the Individual Income Tax

In Michigan in 2005, the income tax provided an exemption of $3,200 per person. Thus, for a Michigan family of four, the personal exemption would shield $3,200 × 4 = $12,800 from income taxes. The personal exemptions mean that Michigan families who are below the poverty line pay very little in state income tax. As a result of the exemptions, the individual income tax in Michigan is progressive at low and middle incomes.

However, the Michigan income tax is not as progressive as the income taxes in most other states, because the income tax in Michigan does not have graduated rates. (There are two main ways to generate progressivity in an income tax. Exemptions can create progressivity at the bottom of the income scale, and graduated rates can continue to impart progressivity at higher levels of income. Most states use both of these features, but Michigan only uses exemptions.) As we move up the income scale, the exemptions are a smaller and smaller percentage of income. Therefore, the Michigan income tax becomes less and less progressive when we consider taxpayers with higher incomes. For example, consider a Michigan family of four with income (before exemptions) of $1,012,800. After the exemptions of $12,800, this family's taxable income will be exactly $1 million. Based on a flat income-tax rate of 3.9 percent, the family will pay $39,000 in Michigan income tax. When we compare this amount of tax to the family's income (before exemptions), their effective average tax rate is about 3.85 percent. For another family with twice as much income, the average effective tax rate would be only barely higher, at about 3.88 percent.

State and local income-tax payments are deductible from the federal individual income tax. This alters the distributional effects of the Michigan income tax for those who itemize deductions on their federal income-tax returns. We will discuss the effects of federal deductibility in a later section of this chapter. In fact, as we shall see, interactions between the Michigan income tax and the federal income tax will eliminate even the tiny amount of progressivity in the high-income ranges that we saw in the preceding paragraph.

The Distributional Effects of Other Taxes

Whereas the income tax is somewhat progressive, at least over a part of the income range, the general retail sales tax is somewhat regressive. This is because the sales tax only applies when people spend their money on taxed goods—i.e., the sales tax does not apply when people save. Since higher-income individuals tend to save more than those with lower incomes, the non-taxation of savings makes the sales tax somewhat regressive. The cigarette tax is also regressive, because smoking is more prevalent among those with lower incomes.[21] On the other hand, the taxes on alcoholic beverages are close to proportional. This is because expenditure on alcohol accounts for about the same percentage of income throughout most of the income range.

The state-run lotteries impose an implicit tax on gamblers, because the lotteries return only a fraction of their gross revenues in prizes. In *Michigan at the Millennium*, Lawrence Martin calculates that the implicit tax rate in the Michigan lotteries is about 60 percent, or ten times as high as the tax rate in the general retail sales tax. As we move up the income scale, there is very little increase, if any, in the amount spent on lottery tickets. Therefore, the *percentage* of income devoted to lottery tickets is highest for those with the lowest incomes. As a result, lotteries are the most regressive source of government revenue.[22]

There is controversy about the effects of property taxes on the distribution of income. If the residential property tax is viewed as a tax on housing, it would be somewhat regressive, because housing accounts for a larger share of income for those with low incomes. If we view the property tax as a tax on capital, it would be somewhat progressive, because high-income taxpayers receive relatively more of their income in the form of capital income, rather than wages and salaries. My reading of the literature is that the more important effect of the property tax is as a tax on capital, so that property taxes are a progressive element of the tax system. For a thorough discussion of this and other aspects of property taxation in Michigan, see the chapter by Naomi Feldman, Paul Courant, and Douglas Drake in *Michigan at the Millennium*.[23]

The Single Business Tax presents special challenges for anyone who would like to determine its effect on different income classes. For one thing, the SBT has a large exemption for small businesses. Thus, the ultimate effects of the SBT depend partly on whether there are differences among consumers of different income classes in the percentage of purchases that come from small businesses and large businesses. This is a subject about which we have very little information. The distributional effects of the SBT also depend on a number of other factors, such as the degree of competitiveness of labor markets and goods markets. James Hines discusses these issues in *Michigan at the Millennium*.

If we put all of these pieces together, on balance, the tax system in Michigan is probably slightly regressive. A study by Robert McIntyre et al.[24] provides comparisons of the distributional effects of the tax systems in the 50 states. Their results should be treated with caution because of the difficulty of assigning taxes to different income classes. Still, it is interesting that they find Michigan to be one of the ten most regressive states in the United States. In other words, when compared with most states, Michigan collects relatively more tax revenues from low-income residents, and relatively fewer tax revenues from high-income residents.

The Increase in Regressivity Over Time

The tax-policy changes of the last 12 years have made the tax system in Michigan more regressive. As we mentioned above, the income tax is progressive, at least over a large part of the income range, whereas the sales tax is somewhat regressive. In 1994, the income-tax rate was reduced and the sales-tax rate was increased. Both of these changes increased the regressivity of the overall tax system. Since 1999, the income-tax rate has been reduced on five more occasions.[25] The only substantial tax *increases* of the last few years have been in the regressive tax on cigarettes.

Michigan's tax system has changed in many ways in the last dozen years, so that any concise summary of the changes must be incomplete. However, as I look at the changes, I see one unifying trend: virtually all of the major changes in the tax law have served to make the tax system more regressive. The persistent theme has been to reduce the taxes on high-income Michigan residents relative to the taxes on those with lower incomes.

The increase in regressivity is especially troublesome because it has occurred against the background of a widening gap between rich and poor. As mentioned in earlier chapters, the distribution of income has become much more unequal in recent decades. The theory of optimal income taxation shows that taxes should be more progressive when the underlying distribution of income is more unequal,[26] but tax policy in Michigan has moved in the opposite direction. At a time when the wages of many low- and middle-income workers have been falling, policy makers have chosen to reduce the taxes on the folks at the top, relative to the taxes on the folks at the bottom.

Of course, income distribution is not the only consideration that should be taken into account when we decide on tax policy. Sound tax policy is based on many considerations, including efficiency and ease of administration, as well as fairness. There are tradeoffs among the various objectives. For example, even though the cigarette tax is regressive, I heartily endorse the recent increases in taxes on cigarettes. Despite its regressivity, the cigarette tax can help to reduce one of the greatest challenges to the health of the American public. Nevertheless, on balance, I believe that the move toward increased regressivity is a step in the wrong direction. I do not advocate a dramatically progressive tax system, but I do believe we should reverse the trend toward greater regressivity. In order to reverse the trend, it would make sense for the income tax to play a more important role, since the income tax is progressive over a large range of incomes.

Tax Exporting

"Tax exporting" occurs when the government of one jurisdiction collects tax revenues that are actually paid by residents of a different jurisdiction. For example, when an Ohio family takes a vacation in Michigan, they will pay some Michigan sales taxes. These sales-tax revenues will go to the State of Michigan, even though Ohio residents actually foot the bill. In this case, we say that Michigan has "exported" some of its taxes to the residents of another state.

Tax exporting can take a variety of forms. In addition to exporting sales taxes through taxes on tourists, some states engage in exporting of income taxes by levying taxes on out-of-state commuters. However, the largest amounts of tax exporting come from the fact that state and local income taxes and property taxes are deductible from the federal individual income tax. For example, let us consider a Michigan family who itemize their deductions in the federal income tax. For every dollar of income tax or property tax that this family pays to a government in Michigan, they get to reduce their federal taxable income by one dollar. This reduces their federal tax liability. The amount of reduction in federal taxes will depend on their tax rate in the federal income tax. If the Michigan family is in the 25 percent federal tax bracket, their federal taxes are reduced by 25 cents for every dollar of state and local income taxes and property taxes. Governments in Michigan get a dollar, but the net cost to the Michigan taxpayer is only 75 cents.[27]

The other 25 cents are effectively exported to taxpayers in the entire country. The federal government might respond in any of several ways to the loss of federal tax revenue that occurs as a result of deductions of Michigan taxes. For example, the federal government might raise other taxes. If so, however, the additional taxes would be paid by people all across the country, and not just by Michigan residents. Alternatively, the federal government might cut services. Once again, however, the cuts would be felt throughout the United States, and not just in Michigan. Finally, the federal government might go further into debt. This would impose a burden on future generations of taxpayers in all 50 states, and not just in Michigan. Thus, although the details will differ depending on the federal government's policies, deductibility means that some Michigan taxes are shifted from Michigan residents to the residents of other states.

Until 1986, the federal income tax offered a deduction for state and local income taxes, property taxes, *and sales taxes*. However, the deduction for state and local sales taxes was removed by the federal Tax Reform Act of 1986.[28] This gave states an incentive to *decrease* their reliance on sales taxes, since sales taxes were no longer deductible. And it also gave states an incentive to *increase* their reliance on income taxes and property taxes, since those taxes were (and still are) deductible. In fact, however, Michigan has done exactly the opposite. When Proposal A was passed in 1994, Michigan lowered its property-tax rates (even though property taxes were still deductible) and greatly increased its sales-tax rate from 4 percent to 6 percent (even though sales taxes were no longer deductible). At the same time, the Michigan income-tax rate was decreased (even though income taxes were still deductible). The income-tax rate has been reduced five more times since Proposal A.

By decreasing income taxes and property taxes, and increasing sales taxes, Michigan is "leaving money on the table." It would be possible for Michigan governments to raise the same amount of tax revenue in Michigan, while sending fewer dollars to the federal government in Washington. But we have chosen not to do so.

The amount of money left on the table is very substantial. According to an estimate by the Office of Revenue and Tax Analysis, Michigan residents paid about $900 million more in federal taxes in 2003 than they would have paid if Proposal A had not been enacted.[29]

Why the Decline in Tax Exporting?

On the basis of the analysis in the last few paragraphs, it is reasonable to ask why some states, including Michigan, have been so reluctant to take advantage of tax exporting. Many explanations are possible. (For a discussion, see Joel Slemrod's chapter in *Michigan at the Millennium*.) One possibility is that the issue of tax exporting has simply been under the radar screen of the public discussion. It certainly appears that tax exporting has played only a very minor role in tax-policy debates in Michigan. Another possibility is that the lack of tax exporting is closely connected to the increased regressivity of the tax system. Those who desire a more regressive tax system have achieved greater political power in the last few decades, and they are willing to leave money on the table if that is what it takes to achieve the goal of greater regressivity. Thus, the amount of money left on the table provides us with a measure of the intensity of the desire to shift more of the tax burden onto the shoulders of low-income residents.

I do not want to overstate the case for tax exporting. It is *not* clear that tax exporting through deductibility is a good policy for the nation as a whole. On the other hand, if the federal government offers Michigan governments the opportunity to export their taxes through deductibility, it is curious that they refuse to take greater advantage of the subsidy.

Tax Exporting and the Rate Structure of Michigan's Income Tax

We have discussed the large increase in income inequality over the last 30 years, and we have also discussed the chronic fiscal crises of governments in Michigan. An increase in Michigan's individual income tax would address both of these problems. An increase in the income tax would raise revenue for cash-strapped governments in Michigan, and it would also reverse the trend toward increasing the proportion of Michigan taxes paid by low-income residents.

Because state and local income taxes are deductible from the federal income tax, a major portion of any increase in Michigan's income tax would be exported. In other words, if we were to increase the Michigan income tax, much of the additional revenue would actually come from residents of other states.

However, income-tax revenues in Michigan can be increased in a variety of ways, and the different methods have very different implications for tax exporting. This is because only about one-third of taxpayers itemize deductions on their federal tax returns, and most itemizers have relatively high incomes. Therefore, if Michigan's income tax were increased, the amount of additional tax exporting would be greater if relatively more of the increase were applied to high-income residents of Michigan. The most effective way to do this would be to introduce graduated rates. My preference is to keep things simple by introducing only one higher tax bracket (although it would also be possible to introduce several additional brackets, as several states have done). However, it should be noted that graduated rates would require an amendment to the Michigan Constitution. Therefore, in political terms, it may be even more difficult to introduce graduated rates than it would be to make some other tax-policy changes. But tax reform is never easy.

If it is not possible politically to introduce graduated rates in the Michigan income tax, I would still advocate other changes in the rate structure of the tax. One possibility is to raise the flat income-tax rate, while keeping the exemption unchanged. This would raise more revenue, some of which would be exported (although a smaller percentage of the additional revenues would be exported than under a system of graduated rates). An increase in the tax rate would also increase the progressivity of the Michigan income tax over a part of the income range.

Another possibility is to increase the personal exemption. This would also increase progressivity, especially at low incomes. However, an increase in the personal exemption would reduce the revenues from the tax, unless offsetting changes were made. In order to avoid exacerbating the budgetary difficulties faced by governments in Michigan, it would be necessary to couple the increase in the exemption with an increase in the income-tax rate.

Before concluding this section, I must reemphasize the fact that tax exporting through federal deductibility is only one consideration in the design of Michigan tax policy. Even if state and local income taxes were not deductible, I would still make the case for greater progressivity in the Michigan income tax, because of my concern about the widening gap between rich and poor. However, in my view, the case for a more progressive income tax in Michigan is strengthened by the availability of tax exporting through federal deductibility.[30]

The Effects of Taxes on the Location of Businesses

Over the years, there has been a great deal of discussion in Michigan of the effects of business taxes (especially the Single Business Tax) on the location of economic activity. It is widely asserted that the SBT is a deterrent to keeping businesses in Michigan. We will discuss the SBT in more detail in the next section. For the moment, however, it makes sense to think about whether the effects of business taxes are large or small.

There is a substantial literature on the effects of taxes on business location. Timothy Bartik of the Upjohn Institute and Leslie Papke of Michigan State University are major contributors to that literature. It is not easy to determine the effects of taxes on business location, because it is necessary to control statistically for a wide variety of influences. There is a lot of variation in the results that emerge from the studies. Some studies do not find that taxes have any effect. However, the consensus is probably that business taxes do have a modest effect, *all else equal*. In a recent paper, Bartik suggests that "a 10 percent decrease in overall state and local business taxes, *holding public services and other location factors constant*, increases the long-term level of economic activity in a state . . . by about 2 percent" (emphasis mine).[31]

Two things need to be said regarding this result about the effect of business taxes. First, this is a fairly small effect. The effect is small because taxes are only one of the many things that go into the decision about where to locate. Sometimes, the advocates of lower business taxes make it sound as if business taxes are the only thing that matters, but that is simply not true. Another statement that one sometimes hears is that a reduction in business taxes would lead to such an amazing burst of economic activity that overall tax revenues would actually increase. In the context of business taxes in Michigan, this idea is mere wishful thinking at best.

Second, when we say that business taxes have an effect, we are making an *all-else-equal* statement. Lower business taxes lead to a slightly higher level of economic activity, *if* everything else (including the level of public services) remains the same. However, if business taxes in Michigan were reduced, not everything else would remain the same. Either other taxes would have to be increased, or public services would have to be reduced. In recent years, the trend in Michigan has been toward cutting taxes, and then reducing the higher-education budget. But in chapter 2 of this book, we emphasized the key role of higher education in economic development. If the SBT were eliminated, and if the resulting loss in revenue were to lead to further cuts in higher-education spending in Michigan, the state's long-term economic prospects would actually be harmed.

A concise summary of these ideas appears in a paper by Michigan State University's Leslie Papke and two of her colleagues:

> The economic effect of taxes tends both to be small and to be less important than other factors. Labor force availability and quality, for example, appear to be more important for explaining differences across locations in economic activity. How tax revenues are spent tends to be important enough that high relative taxes may not be a deterrent to economic growth if the revenues are

used to finance services of value to business, such as education and transportation infrastructure. The studies do make clear that a policy of cutting taxes to induce economic growth is not likely to be efficient or cost-effective.[32]

The Single Business Tax

Now that we have discussed business taxes in general, the next step is to consider Michigan's Single Business Tax in more specific detail. Michigan had a corporate income tax from 1968 to 1975. During those years, the state experienced huge fluctuations in corporate tax-revenue collections. Tax revenues from the Michigan corporate tax fell by about 40 percent between 1969 and 1971. Then, corporate tax revenues doubled between 1971 and 1973, as the economy recovered from the mild recession of the early 1970s. But another recession came, and revenues fell by more than 40 percent between 1973 and 1975. Thus, the corporate tax sent Michigan's fiscal system on a nauseating roller-coaster ride. This is not surprising, since corporate profits have bigger up-and-down swings than other types of income.

Large revenue fluctuations can create major problems for planning and delivering public services. One reason for switching to the Single Business Tax was a desire to get off the revenue roller coaster. In that regard, the SBT has definitely been a success. As shown in James Hines's chapter in *Michigan at the Millennium*, SBT revenues do not soar and dive with the business cycle. Thus, as Hines puts it, the SBT provides "important revenue cushions in years in which the state government has most needed revenues. Other states have found their corporate tax collections moving with the business cycle, thereby exacerbating revenue shortfalls in recession years" (624).

Although revenue stability is an attractive feature, it is not the only consideration in setting tax policy. In some other respects, the SBT does not perform as well. For example, under a tax like the SBT, there will be problems in dealing with the capital investments of firms that do business in many states. Policymakers in Michigan would like to stimulate investments in Michigan, while avoiding subsidies for capital investments in other states. In an attempt to balance these considerations, Michigan adopted a formula for apportioning business deductions for investment in personal property. (Personal property consists primarily of business equipment.) Originally, multi-state companies could take an SBT deduction for a percentage of their total U.S. expenditures on business equipment, where the percentage was determined by the share of U.S. employment and U.S. business property located in Michigan. However, this system was challenged in court. Over time, the tax treatment of business investments in the SBT has been changed repeatedly, although it is not clear that a fully satisfactory solution can be found. (For a description of the complicated history of SBT deductions for business investments, see Hines's chapter in *Michigan at the Millennium*. Also, note that the difficulties in establishing rules for investments by multi-state firms are not confined to the SBT. The same problems are encountered by the states that use corporate taxes.)

Some of the problems of the SBT have more to do with perceptions than with realities. For example, one sometimes hears the objection that the SBT places a heavy burden on small businesses, but this is simply untrue. The SBT contains a very generous exemption for small businesses, so that the overwhelming majority of SBT revenues are paid by large enterprises.

One reason that the SBT may discourage businesses from locating in Michigan is that no other state imposes an SBT. Thus, it is possible that the costs of complying with the tax could keep businesses away from Michigan. In fact, the compliance cost of the SBT is probably no greater than the compliance costs of the corporate taxes in most other states. On the other hand, sometimes perception *is* reality. If businesses *believe* that the cost of complying with the SBT is high, they may avoid doing business in Michigan, even if the *actual* compliance costs are not unusually high.

Nevertheless, it is important to avoid overstating the problems of the SBT. The detractors of the SBT sometimes make exaggerated claims about the economic disincentives caused by the tax. It is true that the SBT (like any other tax) distorts economic decisions. However, as I have emphasized earlier in this chapter, business taxes are only one part of the economic picture. The SBT is not the main cause of Michigan's economic problems, and Michigan will not suddenly become an economic paradise if the SBT is eliminated. The relative decline of manufacturing is a nationwide phenomenon, and it was already well under way before the SBT was even introduced. As shown in chapter 2 of this book, Michigan's population lags behind the national average in terms of educational attainment, and the lack of education cannot be blamed on the SBT. If the SBT had never existed, Michigan's economy would not be dramatically different from the way it is today.

Policy Options for the Single Business Tax

The SBT has been changed in many other ways over the years. In response to a variety of political pressures, lawmakers have approved a dizzying array of exemptions, deductions, and credits. These changes have made the SBT more complex and more inefficient. In 1999, the legislature decided to phase out the SBT, over a period extending to 2020. In 2002, the expiration date for the SBT was moved up to December 31, 2009. Since then, the SBT has continued to be the subject of political wrangling. In March 2006, the legislature passed a measure to move up the elimination of the SBT to October 2007, but without a plan for replacing the revenues. Governor Granholm pledged to veto the measure. As of this writing, an attempt is being made to place a proposal on the ballot under which Michigan voters would eliminate the SBT.

Based on the discussion earlier in this chapter, I hope it is clear that the Single Business Tax has some advantages and some disadvantages. Anyone who reads James Hines's chapter in *Michigan at the Millennium* will see that a solid case can be made for keeping the SBT. However, based on my own assessment of the relative importance of these advantages and disadvantages, I believe the best option is to eliminate the SBT. Removal of the SBT is no panacea. Removal of the SBT will not suddenly solve the problems of the American automobile companies, and it will not suddenly provide Michigan with the kind of highly skilled work force that the future economy will require. Nevertheless, if the SBT were removed, it would be a powerful signal of Michigan's desire for a favorable business climate. No other tax-policy initiative has as much potential to improve Michigan's reputation as a haven for capital investment.[33]

However, if the SBT is eliminated, *it is crucially important to replace the revenues.* If we were to eliminate the SBT and *not* replace it with another source of revenue, an extra shortfall of nearly $2 billion per year would be added to the budget of the State of Michigan, at a time when the state is already experiencing chronic budget crises. This would be fiscally irresponsible in the extreme: the SBT raises about one-fifth of the revenues in the General Fund budget for the State of Michigan. *If the legislature is unwilling to replace the revenue, then the SBT should be kept in place,* and we should focus on getting the SBT to work as smoothly as possible.

Some people suggest that the SBT should be replaced by a corporate income tax, because Michigan "must" have a business tax. But this is a weak argument. There simply is not any rule that a state "has to" have some sort of business tax. Some of the political support for business taxes is based on the misguided impression that businesses are somehow separate from the rest of the economy, and that businesses should pay their "fair share" of taxes. But it really is not meaningful to speak of "business's share" of taxes. Ultimately, taxes are borne by people, in the form of lower wages for workers, or higher prices for consumers, or lower returns on investment for the owners of capital.

The SBT is also sometimes criticized because companies have to pay SBT, even if they are not turning a profit. Once again, this is not a very strong argument. Businesses are required to pay the payroll taxes for their employees' Social Security, Medicare, Disability Insurance, and Unemployment Insurance, regardless of whether they are making a profit. The taxes are just like any other cost of doing business. Retailers are not allowed to skim off a portion of the sales taxes they collect, just because they are not making a profit. This argument is especially weak when it is used to say that we should replace the SBT with a corporate income tax. It is true that a corporate tax would only be paid by businesses that are making a profit. But that fact does not undo all of the other problems associated with corporate taxes.

As we have seen, corporate tax revenues tend to rise and fall dramatically over the business cycle. Therefore, a corporate tax in Michigan can be expected to produce a volatile stream of revenues. This would make it all the more difficult to carry out sensible budget policies. Moreover, a long literature suggests that corporate taxes do an unusually large amount of damage to the economy.[34] A corporate tax is likely to impose greater efficiency costs than the SBT. Just because the SBT has problems, it does not make sense to replace it with something worse. *It would be a mistake to replace the SBT with a corporate income tax. If the only replacement tax acceptable to the legislature is a corporate income tax, then the SBT should be retained.*

If my suggestion is followed, we will eliminate the Single Business Tax, and replace the revenues with something other than a corporate tax. There are plenty of attractive candidates for the source of revenues to replace the SBT. The two that I most prefer are (1) *adding a second rate to the individual income tax*, and (2) *increasing the taxation of services in the sales tax.* Beyond those two possibilities, a number of other potential revenue sources are available. These include plugging some of the holes in the individual income tax, and increasing the tax levels on beer and wine.[35]

In summary, I list the four main options for the Single Business Tax, in order of my assessment of their desirability:

1. Eliminate the SBT, and replace the revenues with something other than a corporate tax, such as an extension of the income tax or the sales tax.
2. Keep the SBT, and strengthen it by removing some of the special deductions, exemptions, and credits that have crept in over the years. This is not a bad option, and it is definitely the best option if #1 is politically infeasible.
3. Replace the SBT with a corporate tax. (This is a bad idea.)
4. Eliminate the SBT, and do not replace it with anything. (This is a *really* bad idea.)

In current policy discussions in Michigan, one sometimes hears the idea of increasing the sales tax to replace not only the SBT but also the income tax and the personal property tax. This is sometimes referred to as the "Fair Tax." One of the most important effects of the "Fair Tax" would be to shift even more taxes away from those with the highest incomes, and to increase the taxes paid by those at the bottom of the income scale. Also, proponents of this type of tax change often drastically understate the tax rates that would be needed to replace the revenue coming from the taxes that are to be eliminated.[36]

Property Taxes

Prior to the enactment of Proposal A in 1994, property taxes in Michigan were based on the "state equalized value" (SEV), which is equal to one-half of the true value of the property. Proposal A instituted the requirement that the taxable value of a property cannot increase in any one year by more than 5 percent or the rate of inflation, whichever is less. Thus, even when the *true* value of a property increases by 8 percent in a year, the *taxable* value cannot increase by more than 5 percent, and the taxable value may increase by only a few percent when the overall rate of inflation is low. (Indeed, the inflation rate has been less than 5 percent per year throughout the entire period since the enactment of Proposal A.) However, when a property is sold, the taxable value reverts to the SEV, and the limitation on the increase of taxable value begins from a new baseline.

This "cap" on taxable value is associated with three important problems. First, the cap reduces the revenue-raising capacity of the property tax at a time when governments in Michigan are subject to chronic fiscal crises. Second, there is an issue of simple fairness. The cap means that two properties can have very different property-tax liabilities, even if they have exactly the same true market value. For example, I have lived in the same house since before Proposal A, and the taxable value of my home is now well below its SEV. But some of my neighbors have only recently moved into the neighborhood. The taxable values of their homes were put back in line with SEV when the homes were purchased. Thus, I pay much less in tax than some of my neighbors, even though the true value of my home is the same as the true value of theirs. Of course, I reap a benefit from this (as long as I stay put). It is easy to understand the political appeal of a provision like this: longtime residents tend to have more political power than those who have recently moved into a community. But the policy is still unfair.

The third problem with the cap on taxable value has to do with economic efficiency. Because of the cap, the effective tax rate on some properties is lower than the effective tax rate on others. It would be more efficient to tax all properties at the same effective rate.

On the basis of these considerations, my conclusion is that the cap on property-tax assessments should be phased out. However, this does not necessarily mean that total property-tax revenues must be increased. As I have said earlier, there is a need for more tax revenues in Michigan. But the additional revenues could come from a variety of sources other than the property tax. If it is desired to keep total property-tax payments relatively unchanged, we could couple the removal of the assessment cap with a reduction of overall property-tax millage rates. However, at the very least, total property-tax revenues should be maintained. If we were to cut property-tax rates so much that total revenues were to fall, it would be grossly irresponsible in these days of structural budget deficits.

The Headlee Amendment and Its Aftermath

We have devoted a great deal of discussion to Proposal A in this chapter. However, Proposal A was not the first landmark change in property taxation in Michigan in the last few decades. The first was the "Headlee Amendment" of 1978. (For a thorough discussion of the Headlee Amendment, see the chapter in *Michigan at the Millennium* by Susan Fino of Wayne State University.) Whereas the assessment cap in Proposal A limits the taxes on *individual properties*, the Headlee Amendment limits the amount of property-tax revenue that can be raised by *jurisdictions*. If the total assessed value of property in a unit of local government increases faster than the Consumer Price Index, there can be an automatic reduction in the property-tax millage rate. This type of tax-rate reduction is known as a "Headlee Rollback."

In the period of nearly 30 years since the passage of the Headlee Amendment, a large number of Headlee Rollbacks have occurred. However, under certain circumstances, a community can avoid being constrained by the Headlee limitations. For example, new construction is excluded from the Headlee calculations. Thus, all else equal, it will be easier for a rapidly growing community to avoid a Headlee Rollback than it would be for a community that is not experiencing much growth. Also, if a community is levying a property-tax millage rate that is less than the maximum allowable rate in a given year, the community has the option of increasing total expenditures beyond the rate of inflation in the following year.

In a recent study, Elisabeth Gerber and Michelle Woolery of the University of Michigan look at the factors determining whether communities are at the maximum allowable property-tax rate.[37] Using data for 87 cities in southeastern Michigan, Gerber and Woolery find that communities with greater property wealth are much less likely to be constrained by the Headlee limitations, all else equal. Their study suggests that in communities where the median home value is greater than $200,000, the probability of being at the maximum allowable property-tax rate is close to zero. On the other hand, the probability of being at the maximum is about 70 percent for communities with a median home value of less than $100,000. Thus, to a major extent, the Headlee limitations perpetuate the inequalities in tax and spending levels that existed in 1978.

The Headlee limitations can interact with the provisions of Proposal A in complicated ways. For a more complete discussion of these interactions, as well as many other aspects of property taxation in Michigan, see the chapter in *Michigan at the Millennium* by Naomi Feldman, Paul Courant, and Douglas Drake.

Summary and Conclusion

In this chapter, I have described the tax systems of state and local governments in Michigan. In several respects, these tax systems are very much like their counterparts in most other states. As in most states, the revenue system is dominated by property taxes, individual income taxes, and general retail sales taxes. In some other respects, however, Michigan's tax system is unusual. When compared with the national average, the *state* government in Michigan collects a substantially higher fraction of the total revenues, while the *local* governments collect less. Another unusual feature is that Michigan's income tax applies a single flat tax rate to all taxable income, instead of using a system of graduated marginal tax rates. Also, Michigan's Single Business Tax is unique among the 50 states.

The level of taxation in Michigan has fallen over the last few decades, and the decreases have been especially rapid in the last seven years. Until recently, the percentage of personal income paid in taxes was slightly higher in Michigan than the national average. However, this is no longer true. In 2003-2004, state and local tax revenues in Michigan were slightly below the national average (even though the national average had dropped substantially since the 1970s). Some of the reductions in tax revenues have been the result of explicit policy changes: over the last 12 years, tax rates have been reduced in the property tax, the individual income tax, and the Single Business Tax. However, most of the tax-revenue reductions have resulted from structural weaknesses in the tax system. For example, the sales tax does not apply to most services. Over the years, services have accounted for a larger and larger fraction of the economy, which means that the revenue losses from nontaxation of services have continued to increase.

Michigan's tax system is one of the most regressive in the country, which means that a relatively large share of taxes in Michigan is borne by low-income residents. Moreover, the Michigan tax system has become more regressive over time: individual income taxes have been reduced, while the regressive sales tax has been increased.

Michigan has increased its reliance on the sales tax, even though sales taxes are not deductible from the federal individual income tax. On the other hand, Michigan has reduced the rates of its income and property taxes, even though these taxes are deductible. This means that Michigan has reduced the extent to which it "exports" its taxes to the residents of other states. In fact, taxpayers in Michigan pay hundreds of millions of extra federal taxes every year, as a result of the shift from deductible taxes to nondeductible taxes.

Any change in tax policy will face major political obstacles. Nevertheless, it is imperative to think anew about taxes in Michigan. The current tax system has serious structural problems, which we ignore at our peril. If nothing is done to address these problems, the Michigan tax system will become more inefficient, and it will become increasingly unable to finance an appropriate level of public services. Thus, based on the analysis in this chapter, I have identified a number of tax-policy changes that deserve very serious consideration. The first and foremost need is to reverse the steady decline of tax revenues in Michigan. It makes the most sense to do this in ways that also help to achieve other objectives for the tax system, such as economic efficiency and fairness. The following proposals would raise revenue, while also improving the tax system in other ways:

- *Adding a second tax bracket in the individual income tax.* Michigan is one of only a few states that have an income tax with only a single tax rate. Of the 43 states with an income tax, 37 have a system of graduated marginal tax rates, with higher rates on those with higher incomes. A second tax rate would raise additional revenue, and it would also go against the recent trend of putting more of the tax burden on the low-income residents of Michigan. Moreover, some of the additional income-tax revenues would actually be borne by the residents of other states, as a result of the deductibility of state and local income taxes in the federal income tax. If it proves politically impossible to introduce graduated marginal tax rates in Michigan, we can still move part of the way by increasing the single tax rate in the income tax. This could be accompanied by an increase in the personal exemption. However, in the current budgetary climate, it would be inappropriate to increase the personal exemption without also increasing the income-tax rate.
- *Taxing services.* The general retail sales tax in Michigan applies to a few serv-

ices, but a great deal of the service economy is untaxed, even though services have been steadily increasing in relative importance for decades. If more services are taxed, the revenue-raising capability of the tax system will be reinforced. Just as important, more complete taxation of services will make the sales tax more efficient and more equitable.

- *Reducing the tax preferences for the elderly in the income tax.* The income tax in Michigan provides extraordinary tax breaks for elderly residents. As a result, very few senior citizens in Michigan pay any income tax. On net, Michigan seniors actually pay *negative* amounts of income tax. The revenue losses associated with these tax breaks are expected to grow substantially as the Baby Boom generation enters retirement. If the taxation of senior citizens were brought more into line with the patterns of taxation in other states, it would help to preserve the integrity of the tax system.

- *Changing the taxation of beer, wine, tobacco products, diesel fuel, and gasoline.* Currently, these taxes are levied on a *per-unit* basis. When taxes operate in this manner, their revenue-raising capacity is eroded over time by inflation. The unit taxes on beer and wine in Michigan have remained the same for decades, even though inflation has pushed prices dramatically higher. Therefore, the effective tax rates on beer and wine have decreased greatly. If these tax rates were raised, and then converted to a percentage basis, it would help to shore up the revenue system, and it would also help to discourage irresponsible drinking. It would also be a good idea to convert the taxes on tobacco products and motor fuels to a percentage basis. In addition, Michigan is unusual in that the tax on diesel fuel is lower than the gasoline tax. An increase in the tax rate on diesel fuel would raise additional revenue at the same time that it eliminates the inequitable treatment of drivers of different vehicle types.

- *Removing the "assessment cap" in the property tax.* Since the passage of Proposal A, the *taxable* value of any individual property cannot increase in one year by more than the overall rate of inflation or 5 percent, whichever is less (even if the *market* value of the property increases by more). However, properties are reassessed at full value when sold. As a result, two adjacent properties can have very different property-tax bills, even if they have exactly the same market value. If the assessment cap were removed, this inequity would be removed along with it, and additional revenue would be raised. If there is a desire to avoid a sudden spike in property taxes, the elimination of the cap could be phased in gradually, and it could be accompanied by an overall reduction in property-tax rates. However, such a rate reduction should not be too large, or it would merely exacerbate Michigan's budgetary problems.

Finally, policy makers in Michigan must decide what to do with the Single Business Tax. There is little doubt that the SBT is an improvement upon the corporate income tax, which it replaced in 1975. Nevertheless, the SBT has encountered a number of problems, especially in the tax treatment of business investments. Over the years, the SBT has become riddled with deductions and exemptions. Currently, the SBT is a few years away from scheduled elimination.

In my judgment, the best policy would be to eliminate the SBT. However, if the SBT is to be eliminated, it must be replaced with *something*. To eliminate the SBT and *not* replace it would be fiscally irresponsible to an astonishing degree. If the legislature is unwilling to replace the lost revenues, then the SBT should be kept in place. Moreover, we cannot replace the SBT with just anything. If the SBT is removed and replaced, it should *not* be replaced with a corporate income tax. The best sources of revenues to replace the Single Business Tax are the individual income tax and the general retail sales tax.

NOTES

1. The states with no income tax are Alaska, Florida, Nevada, South Dakota, Texas, Washington, and Wyoming.

2. Delaware, Montana, New Hampshire, and Oregon have no retail sales taxes.

3. Table 5.1 is based on information from the Census of Governments for 2003–2004.

4. As of January 1, 2005, the cigarette-tax rate in Michigan is $2 per pack, the third-highest in the country, behind the rates of $2.46 per pack in Rhode Island and $2.40 per pack in New Jersey. (These data are from the Federation of Tax Administrators, at *http://www .taxadmin.org/fta/rate/cigarett.html*.) This contrasts with rates of less than 10 cents per pack in Kentucky, North Carolina, and South Carolina.

5. In 1992, about 3.7 percent of the property taxes in Michigan were collected by the state government. By 2004, state property taxes accounted for about 17.5 percent of the property taxes collected in Michigan.

6. In addition to Michigan, five other states have a flat-rate income tax. These are Colorado, Illinois, Indiana, Massachusetts, and Pennsylvania. Details on the income-tax rates in the various states are available at *http://www.taxadmin.org/fta/rate/ind_inc.html*.

7. The personal exemptions in the individual income tax also have an effect on the distribution of the tax burden among people of different income classes. As of January 1, 2005, some 31 states used a personal exemption. The personal exemption for a married couple is larger in Michigan than in 19 of these states, and smaller than in 11 of them. Seven states use a credit in lieu of a personal exemption. The effective dollar value of these credits is larger than the personal exemption in Michigan in some cases, and smaller in others.

8. In addition to Michigan, the states without a corporate income tax are Nevada, Texas, Washington, and Wyoming.

9. For all of the years from 1992 to 2000, as well as for 2002 and 2004, annual data are available at the Census Bureau website, at *http://www.census.gov/govs/www/estimate.html*. For 1972, 1977, 1982, and 1987, the data are taken from the Census of Governments, vol. 4, no. 5, "Compendium of Government Finances." In constructing figure 5.1, the years between 1972 and 1977, 1977 and 1982, 1982 and 1987, 1987 and 1992, ,2000 and 2002, and 2002 and 2004 were interpolated. For more on calculations of this type, see my report "Michigan's Tax Climate: A Closer Look," prepared for the Michigan Chamber Foundation, April 2004.

10. See "Executive Budget, Fiscal Year 2006," available at *http://www.michigan.gov/documents/ FY05Document1_84532_7.pdf*.

11. When tax rates are reduced, there will usually be an increase in economic activity, all else equal. Thus, all else equal, a reduction in tax rates will usually lead to an increase in the tax base. This means that the decrease in tax *revenues* will be relatively smaller than the decrease in tax *rates*. However, the increase in economic activity will not usually be large enough to lead to an increase in tax revenues.

12. See *http://www.michigan.gov/documents/ExFY2004_59269_7.pdf*.

13. For a very readable discussion of the possibility of taxing more services, along with commentary from several current and former public officials, see the article by Stacey Range and Chris Andrews in the *Lansing State Journal*, October 16, 2005.

14. The tax rate that would raise the same amount of revenue would depend on how many items were brought into the tax base. However, as mentioned above, an efficient tax system would not involve taxes on business-to-business sales. Thus, if a tax reform is to be carried out in the best way, it cannot merely tax everything in sight.

15. To further reinforce my point about job losses, I offer this analogy: Suppose that people with family names beginning with the letter "B" were exempt from paying the income tax

and the payroll tax. This would obviously be a huge advantage for people like me, but that does not make it good tax policy. It would be both inequitable and inefficient. If it were then proposed to eliminate the privileged treatment of the B's, it is easy to imagine B's arguing that the reform would reduce employment of B's. In fact, it is very possible that B employment would be reduced by the reform, but that is not the end of the story. Employment of folks with names beginning with other letters would likely increase, because they would no longer be penalized by the tax system.

16. As pointed out by Paul Menchik in *Michigan at the Millennium*, the inflation-adjusted value of the personal exemption is now only about half as large as it was when the Michigan income tax was established in the late 1960s.

17. The tax on cigarettes in Michigan was raised from 75 cents per pack to $1.25 per pack in 2002, and then to $2.00 per pack in 2004.

18. This calculation is based on the Implicit Price Deflator for Personal Consumption Expenditures, available from table 1.1.4 on the website of the Bureau of Economic Analysis, U.S. Department of Commerce, at *http://www.bea.gov/bea/dn/nipaweb/SelectTable.asp?Selected=N*. If we use the Consumer Price Index, the increase of the price level from 1962 to 2005 is even steeper, at about 550 percent. For technical reasons, I prefer to use the Personal Consumption Expenditures deflator. However, either of these inflation measures makes it clear that the price level has risen a great deal in the last 40-plus years.

19. Of course, taxes on alcoholic beverages are a fairly blunt method for discouraging excessive drinking, since the tax on the casual drinker is levied at the same rate as the tax on the binge drinker. It is important to enforce the drunk-driving laws, regardless of the tax rate on alcoholic beverages. There is evidence that the optimal fine for a drunk-driving arrest should be very high. (See Steven Levitt and Jack Porter, "How Dangerous are Drinking Drivers?" *Journal of Political Economy* 109 [2001]: 1198-1237.)

20. These data are from the website of the Federation of Tax Administrators, at *http://www.tax-admin.org/fta/rate/motor_fl.html*.

21. See Lawrence Martin's chapter in *Michigan at the Millennium* for an extensive discussion of the effects of the cigarette tax on the distribution of income. The economist Jonathan Gruber has advanced a novel argument suggesting that the cigarette tax is not regressive, but Gruber's perspective is still controversial. In this discussion, I will maintain the traditional view that cigarette taxes are regressive.

22. See Lawrence Martin's chapter in *Michigan at the Millennium*. Charles Clotfelter and Philip Cook provide an overview of the economic issues associated with lotteries in "On the Economics of State Lotteries," *Journal of Economic Perspectives* 4 (1990): 105–119.

23. Paul Courant is with the University of Michigan. Douglas Drake was with Wayne State

University when *Michigan at the Millennium* was written, but he is now with Public Policy Associates. Naomi Feldman was with the University of Michigan when *Michigan at the Millennium* was written; she is now at Ben-Gurion University of the Negev.

24. Robert McIntyre, Robert Denk, Norton Francis, Matthew Gardner, Will Gomaa, Fiona Hsu, and Richard Sims, "Who Pays? A Distributional Analysis of the Tax Systems in All 50 States," 2nd edition (Washington, D.C.: Institute on Taxation and Economic Policy, 2003).

25. A reduction in the tax rate is not the only way to reduce the revenues from the income tax. Another possibility would be to increase the personal exemption. These two methods of tax reduction have different effects on the distribution of income. An increase in the exemption would be relatively more favorable for low- and middle-income families, whereas rate reductions are relatively better for those with higher incomes. Since the recent income-tax changes have focused on rate reductions, rather than on increases in the personal exemption, they are consistent with the overall trend toward increased regressivity.

26. For example, see Nicholas Stern, "On the Specification of Models of Optimum Income Taxation," *Journal of Public Economics* 6 (1976): 123–162.

27. Earlier in this chapter, we discussed the effect of the Michigan income tax on the distribution of income. The income tax is somewhat progressive at low incomes, because of the personal exemptions. For middle incomes, the tax is approximately proportional, because it has only a single flat rate. However, because of deductibility, the net effect of the Michigan income tax is actually somewhat regressive at high incomes. For example, consider a married couple with $60,000 of federal taxable income in 2004. This family would have been in the 25 percent federal tax bracket. When the couple paid a dollar of Michigan income tax, they would save 25 cents of federal tax, so their net payment would be 75 cents. On the other hand, a couple with $320,000 of federal taxable would have been in the 35 percent federal bracket. When this couple paid a dollar of Michigan income tax, their net payment would be only 65 cents. One other complication bears noting. The federal income tax includes an "Alternative Minimum Tax" (AMT). When it was instituted in 1969, the AMT was targeted at a very small number of taxpayers, with very high incomes, who had taken advantage of special provisions of the tax code to avoid paying any federal income tax. However, the AMT is not adjusted for inflation, and the AMT rules have not been adjusted to keep pace with other tax-policy changes. Hence, unless the law is changed, the number of taxpayers affected by the AMT is expected to skyrocket in the next few years. The AMT is relevant to tax exporting because AMT liability can be triggered by deductions for state and local taxes. If the deductions cause "too much" of a reduction in a taxpayer's regular federal income-tax liability, the taxpayer may have to pay

AMT. Thus, one effect of the AMT is to create a back-door method of reducing the effect of the deduction for state and local taxes. If the AMT is not changed, it could significantly reduce the extent of tax exporting through federal deductibility. However, it is possible that the AMT may be reduced or eliminated. President Bush's Advisory Panel on Tax Reform has recommended abolition of the AMT (although it remains to be seen whether this recommendation will be enacted).

28. Recently, the deduction for state and local sales taxes was partly reinstated. Taxpayers can now deduct either their state and local income taxes, or their sales taxes, but not both. As a practical matter, this will have very little effect on Michigan taxpayers. Its greatest effect will be for taxpayers in states like Florida and Texas, which do not have an income tax.

29. See "School Finance Reform in Michigan: Proposal A: Retrospective," available at *http://www.michigan.gov/documents/propa_3172_7.pdf*.

30. President Bush's Advisory Panel on Tax Reform has proposed to eliminate the deductions for state and local taxes. (See Robert Guy Matthews, "Tax-Overhaul Panel Gives Bush Two Choices," *Wall Street Journal*, October 19, 2005.) However, the fate of this proposal is uncertain. The political obstacles to federal tax reform are well known, and many analysts have expressed doubt that the panel's recommendations will be adopted soon.

31. See Timothy Bartik, "Michigan's Business Taxes and Economic Development: Possible Reforms" (February 14, 2006), available at *http://www.upjohninst.org/TJB_testimony_2-17-06.pdf*.

32. See Stephen T. Mark, Therese J. McGuire, and Leslie E. Papke, "What Do We Know about the Effect of Taxes on Economic Development? Lessons from the Literature for the District of Columbia," *State Tax Notes*, August 25, 1997.

33. Of course, if the SBT were eliminated, it would no longer be possible to offer SBT abatements for particular proposed investments. On balance, however, there are many advantages to having no SBT, rather than having an SBT with more special provisions. Also, SBT abatements are not the only way to try to attract businesses. For example, it would still be possible to offer reductions in the personal-property tax for new businesses and/or expanding businesses. For a discussion of the vast array of tools used to promote economic development in Michigan, see the chapter in *Michigan at the Millennium* by Timothy Bartik, Peter Eisinger, and George Erickcek.

34. Classic contributions to this literature include Arnold Harberger, "Efficiency Effects of Taxes on Income from Capital," in Marion Krzyzaniak, ed., *Effects of the Corporation Income Tax* (Detroit: Wayne State University Press, 1966); and John Shoven, "The Incidence and Efficiency Effects of Taxes on Income from Capital," *Journal of Political Economy* 84 (1976): 1261–1283.

35. The taxes mentioned in this section provide revenue for the state government, rather than local governments. However, it would certainly be possible to arrange for some portion of the revenues to go directly to local governments.

36. For discussion, see William G. Gale and Janet Holtzblatt, "The Role of Administrative Issues in Tax Reform: Simplicity, Compliance, and Administration," in George R. Zodrow and Peter Mieszkowski, eds., *United States Tax Reform in the 21st Century* (Cambridge and New York: Cambridge University Press, 2002).

37. See Elisabeth Gerber and Michelle Woolery, "Federalism and Equality: The Impact of State Fiscal Policies on Local Governments," working paper, University of Michigan, November 2005.

What Will Michigan's Economy
Be Like in 2025?

O n December 1, 1862, in the midst of the greatest crisis in U.S. history, Abraham Lincoln sent his second annual message to Congress. He wrote, "The dogmas of the quiet past are inadequate to the stormy present. The occasion is piled high with difficulty, and we must rise with the occasion. As our case is new, so we must think anew, and act anew. We must disenthrall ourselves, and then we shall save our country."

The difficulties facing the people of Michigan today are not nearly as profound as the difficulties faced by Lincoln and his fellow citizens during the Civil War. Nevertheless, Michigan is at a critical moment in its history. We too face an occasion that is piled high with difficulty, and we too must rise to the occasion. We in Michigan in 2006 would do well to heed Lincoln's words: yesterday's dogmas are inadequate for today. If Michigan's economy is to reverse the long, slow slide of the last several decades, we will need *new attitudes* and *new policies*. In this book, I have discussed attitudes and policies that I believe will help lead to a brighter economic future for Michigan.

In the title of this final chapter, I ask what Michigan will be like in the year 2025 (rather than 2007 or 2008 or 2009). I frame the question in this way because Michigan faces *long-term* economic problems. These problems will not be fixed in the next year or two, or even in the next four years. However, if the people of Michigan have the wisdom and courage to do something about it, we can make some major improvements over the longer term.

Much of this chapter will be devoted to a summary and synthesis of the policy analysis from the earlier chapters. However, before I get to that summary and synthesis, I want to say a few words about the *values* that have formed the basis of the policy recommendations in this book. People with different values can look at the same set of facts and reach different policy conclusions. Thus, the policy recommendations discussed here are not merely the result of my economic analysis; they are also the result of my values.

Values Regarding Future Generations of Michigan Residents

As I see it, the people of today have an obligation to pave the way to a decent future for the people of tomorrow. Unfortunately, many of the decisions being made today, in Michigan and across the country, are doing a disservice to the people of future generations. For example, the private savings rate in the United States has been declining for decades. And, except for the brief period from 1997 to 2000, the federal government has run large budget deficits for more than a generation. Consequently, Americans are now borrowing half a *trillion* dollars per year from other countries. Americans are spending like there's no tomorrow.

While we are on the subject of behaving like there's no tomorrow, Michigan is cutting its investment in higher education. At this crucial moment, we in Michigan are eating our seed corn.

I believe these trends are taking us in the wrong direction. The problem with behaving like there's no tomorrow is that tomorrow will come, whether we prepare for it or not. To use the jargon of economists, my values include not "discounting" the future very greatly. But those who discount the future very heavily may look at today's situation and say that everything is fine. Many of my recommendations will not make much sense to those who place far more weight on today than on tomorrow.

Values Regarding Middle-Income and Low-Income Residents of Michigan

The second set of values that must be mentioned are values concerning the distribution of income. I am troubled by the increasing inequality of income and wealth, in Michigan and throughout the United States. Those with the most education and skill have done extraordinarily well in the last few decades, while many of the rest of Michigan's people have lost ground. Personally, I have benefited from the increase in the rewards to skill. And, as I said in an earlier chapter, some inequality is necessary to give people an incentive to work hard and get an education. However, the trend toward greater inequality has pushed very, very far in the last few decades. In my view, it has gone too far.

Once again, however, not everyone shares my values in this regard. Many of the recommendations in this book probably will not make much sense to those who have relatively little concern for the people on the lower rungs of the economic ladder. Many of my recommendations will not make sense to those who desire to see a wider gap between rich and middle class, and a wider gap between middle class and poor. I have recommended that Michigan should spend more on various aspects of K–12 education. From the perspective of the affluent few who can easily afford private-school tuition, this may not seem very reasonable. I have also recommended that we ensure that all schoolchildren in Michigan are educated in adequate facilities, including even those children who live in poor communities. Again, from the perspective of some folks in affluent suburban enclaves, this may not make sense. I have also recommended greater state support for public colleges and universities. But this may seem strange to those who can easily afford to send their sons and daughters to expensive private colleges. I have recommended that the income tax in Michigan should be made more progressive. But some affluent Michigan residents may ask why we should do this: Why shouldn't we do as much as possible to put the tax burden on the shoulders of the middle-income and low-income people of Michigan, and to reduce the tax burden for the most affluent?

It is commonplace to say that Michigan's economy is not performing very well. I have said as much on several occasions in this book. But we need to keep in mind that this is a statement about the Michigan economy *as a whole*. For the most affluent folks in Michigan, the economy has performed astonishingly well. The incomes of the top 20 percent have skyrocketed. At the same time, the state and local tax system in Michigan has been changed repeatedly, in ways that reduce the taxes of those at the top while increasing the taxes of middle-income and low-income Michigan residents. These policies are consistent with a philosophy that has relatively little concern for the people in the bottom 80 percent of the income distribution in Michigan.

Of course, few people will say out loud that they want the rich to get richer and the poor to get poorer. And few will say out loud that they don't care very much about the people of future generations. But actions speak louder than words. If one looks at Michigan's economic policies of the last few decades, one sees a pattern that fits with values that are very different from the values I have espoused here. The pattern of recent economic policy in Michigan is consistent with a set of values that places relatively little emphasis on the needs of the people of future generations, or the people in the bottom 80 percent of the income distribution.

One more point must be made before I move on to the summary and synthesis. Throughout this book, I have repeatedly emphasized the crucial role played by higher education in the knowledge-driven, skills-intensive economy of the future. I am also an employee of a research university that receives support from the state government. Some people may look at my advocacy for higher education and see nothing but my own selfish interests. Obviously, there is no way for me to refute conclusively the charge that I am merely trying to feather my own nest. But I can at least say a few things about it. First, speaking as objectively as I possibly can, I honestly believe I would say the same things even if I did not work for Michigan State University. The ideas advanced here are strong ideas, regardless of what happens to me personally. Moreover, if people were disqualified from speaking out on subjects in which they themselves have an interest, our public debates would be very quiet indeed.

Key Features of the Economic Situation in Michigan

This book covers a very wide range of economic issues facing the people of Michigan. However, four aspects of Michigan's economic situation are of central importance:

• *Manufacturing has been declining, and will continue to decline.* As a percentage of the economy, manufacturing has been shrinking for decades, both in Michigan and in the rest of the country. However, in chapter 1, we saw that manufacturing accounts for a much larger share of the economy in Michigan than in the United States as a whole. Thus, the transition out of manufacturing is more difficult for Michigan than for most other parts of the country.

The largest manufacturing industry in Michigan is the automobile industry, which has special problems. In particular, the Michigan auto industry is dominated by the Big Three domestic auto companies, which have fared much worse than the industry as a whole. These companies are saddled with a cost structure that is unsustainable in today's competitive environment. As a result, the Big Three have been losing market share and shrinking their work forces for many years. Those Michigan workers who have been fortunate enough to keep jobs in the auto industry have done extremely well, but the level of auto-industry employment in Michigan has shrunk significantly. Many of Michigan's economic difficulties can be traced, directly or indirectly, to the heavy reliance on manufacturing, and on automobiles in particular.

Manufacturing was the foundation of Michigan's tremendous economic success in the middle of the twentieth century. Although manufacturing will remain important to the Michigan economy for many years to come, there is no reason to believe that it will return to the dominance it enjoyed 50 years ago. The old days are gone, and they aren't coming back.

• *The future belongs to people with skill, but Michigan's education system has fallen short of what is needed.* The evolving global economy is centered on highly skilled, highly educated, creative people. Unfortunately, as discussed in chapter 2, Michigan's education system is not delivering enough workers who can best take advantage of the new economic realities. Achievement scores for elementary and secondary students are very close to the national average. It would be good to be close to the national average if the national average were impressive, but the national average is pathetic.

The proportion of Michigan's adult population with a college degree has lagged substantially below the national average for many years. This may have made sense in the heyday of manufacturing, when a young man with only a high-school diploma had a good chance of getting a highly paid factory job. The economic realities of yesteryear are long gone, but unfortunately the old attitudes linger on. Thus, too many of Michigan's people are inadequately prepared for the high-tech, high-skill jobs of the future. And yet the budget for higher education has been cut dramatically.

Michigan has had some successes in the field of industrial high technology, but these have not yet been large enough to turn around the overall

economy. The old manufacturing base has been declining, but the knowledge-driven sectors of the future have not grown rapidly enough to make up
the losses. As a result, when compared with the United States average, per
capita income in Michigan has fallen by about 15 percent in the last 50 years.

• *Incomes have become dramatically more unequal.* As mentioned above, Michigan lags behind the national average in the portion of its adult population
with a college degree. However, those who *do* have a college education have
fared extraordinarily well in the last 30 years. After adjusting for inflation, the
labor-market earnings of Michigan workers with a college degree have
soared. The earnings of people with a high-school diploma have fallen
slightly, and the earnings of people with less than a high-school education
have plummeted. As a result, the income gap has widened a great deal. In
Michigan, and in the rest of the United States, the degree of inequality has
now climbed to levels not seen since the early part of the twentieth century.

• *Tax revenues have shrunk.* At one time, taxes in Michigan were above the
national average, but that is no longer true. As a proportion of personal income, state and local tax revenues in Michigan have declined fairly steadily for
more than 30 years. If state and local taxes in Michigan were at the average
level of the last generation, they would bring in about $5 billion per year more
than they actually bring in now.

Some of the reductions in tax revenues have been caused by explicit cuts
in tax rates. However, most of the revenue losses are caused by structural
weaknesses in the tax system. As discussed in chapter 5, these weaknesses can
be found in the income tax, the property tax, the sales tax, and the excise
taxes on beer, wine, motor fuels, and tobacco products. In other words, *every
important revenue source for state and local governments in Michigan has serious structural problems.* As a result, the taxed portion of the economy has diminished
substantially over the years. The tax system's ability to raise revenues has
been seriously eroded, and the state and local governments in Michigan are in
a state of chronic fiscal crisis.

Finally, all of the major changes in Michigan's tax system have put more of
the burden of taxes onto people with low and moderate incomes, while those
with high incomes have been privileged to pay a declining share of the taxes.

Of course, the four trends discussed in the preceding paragraphs are
not the only things going on with Michigan's economy. In my opinion, however, these four interrelated trends are the most important forces shaping the

economy. If the people of Michigan understand these trends clearly, they will have taken an important first step toward a brighter economic future.

On the basis of the analysis of these and other trends, I have included a number of policy suggestions in this book. I conclude with a brief review of these ideas for improving economic policy in Michigan.

K–12 Education Policies

Michigan is underinvested in every single part of the educational system, from preschool to Ph.D. If the people of Michigan are going to make long-term economic improvements, their top priority should be to increase the skill level of the population. I developed several recommendations for Michigan's K–12 educational system in chapter 2 of this book.

- *Continue to provide adequate funding for operating expenses for every school district, while allowing individual school districts to provide more if they wish.* Proposal A, passed in 1994, led to very substantial increases in funding for the lowest-spending school districts in Michigan. This was a great achievement, and it has led to improvements in educational outcomes. The state government should ensure that the funding for the lowest-spending school districts is maintained at an adequate level. However, funding for the higher-spending school districts has grown much less rapidly, if at all. Steps should be taken to allow these districts to spend more on schools, if their voters desire to do so.
- *Provide additional state funding for capital expenditures for public schools.* Since the passage of Proposal A, the funding for *operating* expenses for the public schools has not depended on local property taxes. However, *capital* expenditures still rely almost exclusively on local property taxes. Consequently, the poorest school districts in Michigan are unable to provide adequate physical facilities for their students, even though many of them have high property-tax rates. The state government should assume a much larger share of the financial responsibility for capital expenditures, with the near-term goal of ensuring that every student in Michigan goes to school in a physical environment that is safe, modern, and educationally sound.
- *Shift more of the financial responsibility for pensions and medical care for retired*

teachers to the state government. Currently, the individual school districts in Michigan are responsible for these pension and health-care obligations. These costs have been rising rapidly, and they are expected to increase even more rapidly in the next 15 years. These escalating costs have already forced many school districts to make painful cuts in services. If nothing is done, the school districts will have to make even more severe cuts in the near future.

• *Increase the amount of instruction.* Today's school calendar, with a three-month summer break, is better suited to the economic needs of 100 years ago than to the needs of today. In chapter 2, I discussed a number of ways in which the amount of instruction could be increased. One of these is to lengthen the school year, perhaps to 190 or 195 days. If this is done, it would be important not to offset the change by increasing the number of "half days." Another policy would involve increasing the age of compulsory school attendance from 16 to 17, or perhaps even to 18. Yet another would be to require (or at least encourage) school districts to increase their use of full-day kindergarten programs.

Higher Education Policies

In addition to the discussion of K–12 education, chapter 2 of this book also included a discussion of higher education. Several recommendations emerged.

• *Reverse the trend toward reduced state support for community colleges and universities.* In chapter 2, we discussed the strong effect of post-high-school education on productivity and earnings. The wage premium for a college education has grown sharply in the last 30 years. Moreover, the research universities provide other benefits for the state through a wide variety of channels, such as bringing in federal research dollars. And yet, Michigan has been reducing its financial support for institutions of higher learning. This shortsighted strategy must be reversed.

• *Ensure access to higher education for students from middle-income and low-income Michigan families.* Young people from families of modest means are the ones most likely to be unable to attend college for financial reasons. Policies regarding tuition and financial aid should give strong consideration to financial need. The goal should be to make sure that no talented young person in Michigan is prohibited from attending college because of cost.

Economic-Development Policies

If Michigan is to have a successful economic-development strategy, it is very important to understand that some widely touted policies will *not* get us where we need to go. In the policy debate regarding economic development in Michigan, it is often suggested that taxes play a huge role, and that business tax cuts have almost magical effects. But the decisions of real-world businesses actually depend on many things other than taxes. In fact, business taxes are well down the list of criteria that businesses use when making decisions about where to locate.

Real-world businesses do pay attention to taxes. But they also pay attention to the availability of skilled workers, and to the wages that must be paid to attract those workers, and to transportation infrastructure, and to access to natural resources, and to the availability of cultural and recreational amenities, and to many other factors.

In this book, I have suggested that Michigan should repeal the Single Business Tax (SBT). This might seem inconsistent with my statements about the modest effects of taxes. In fact, I really do believe that Michigan's economy could be improved if we were to replace the Single Business Tax, but our expectations should be realistic. Repeal of the SBT will not lead to a dramatic transformation of the Michigan economy. The long-term structural problems of Michigan's economy are large enough that repeal of the SBT will only have a modest effect. The most important point is that the SBT should only be repealed *if the revenues are fully replaced*. Taxes in Michigan have been cut, and cut, and cut again. This has led to repeated and very substantial cuts in some areas of the budget (although not in corrections). If we were to engage in even more tax cuts, it would further erode our ability to deliver essential public services. We could expect more deterioration of our roads, our parks, and, most critically, our schools, colleges, and universities. In the long run, the best strategy for economic development is to have a highly skilled work force, and a single-minded fixation on tax cuts will not help. If we put excessive faith in tax cuts, it can blind us to the real issues in economic development.

Michigan already has a very substantial economic-development program. In many ways, our economic-development efforts are solid. It is true that the overall performance of the Michigan economy has been mediocre, but this is primarily due to other factors, and not to the lack of economic-development efforts. Still, those efforts could be improved. It would help to have greater consistency over time in economic-development policies, and it would help to undertake periodic outside reviews in order to assess the effectiveness of the existing programs and to suggest new ones.

The biggest problem with economic development for Michigan has to do with attitudes rather than with programs. Fifty years ago, Michigan's economy was the envy of the world. We were so successful that we became complacent. We thought the good times would last forever, and that the world would always come knocking on our door. More than anything else, we need to snap out of our nostalgia, and recognize that today's highly competitive global economic environment demands that we market ourselves more aggressively than ever before. More than ever before, we need to redouble our efforts to provide "one-stop shopping" for businesses, with integrated assistance with site location, infrastructure, and training.

Transportation Policies

In chapter 3, we considered Michigan's physical resources, including transportation. Several recommendations came out of that discussion.

- *Reallocate state highway funds.* The roads in Michigan are of poorer quality than the roads in neighboring states. The problems are especially severe in urban areas. One reason for this is that highway funds in Michigan are allocated on the basis of a formula that is extremely biased in favor of sparsely populated rural counties. The formula should be changed, so as to increase the funding for roads in the urban areas that contain the vast majority of Michigan's people. This would be both more equitable and more efficient.
- *Provide for state ownership of a larger fraction of the major highways in Michigan.* In most states, the state highway authority owns most of the major highways. However, the Michigan Department of Transportation owns

relatively few of the major roads, most of which are owned by county road commissions. This may also contribute to the fact that Michigan's lightly traveled rural roads are in relatively better shape than its urban highways.

- *Consider stricter truck weight limits.* The weight limits for trucks are far higher in Michigan than in the rest of the country. There is a good possibility that ultraheavy trucks do an unusually large amount of damage to the roads. Thus, Michigan should consider adopting weight limits that are more in line with those in the rest of the United States. At a minimum, more scientific research should be undertaken to improve our understanding of the damage done to roads by heavy trucks.
- *Increase the taxes on gasoline and diesel fuel, with a larger increase on diesel fuel.* Currently, Michigan is one of only a few states in which the tax rate on diesel fuel is lower than the tax rate on gasoline. The diesel tax should be increased so that it is at least equal to the gasoline tax. In addition, the condition of Michigan's roads is so poor that reallocation of the existing funds will not be enough to get the roads into adequate shape. An increase in both the gasoline tax and the diesel-fuel tax can help to raise the needed revenue.
- *Consider greater use of tolls.* Tolls can raise revenue for road construction and maintenance. Also, tolls can help to spread out the volume of traffic, thus increasing the effective capacity of the existing roads. Michigan has never made substantial use of tolls, but they are proving increasingly effective in other states and other countries. Thus, a strong case can be made for increasing the use of tolls in Michigan.

Land-Use Policies

If Michigan's economic-development policies are successful in attracting more businesses, there will be increased pressure to develop land for industrial, commercial, and residential uses. Even if the Michigan economy continues to grow slowly, land use will continue to be hotly contested. Much of the controversy involves the density of development. In recent decades, the population density of metropolitan areas has been decreasing, in Michigan and in the rest of the United States. In Michigan, even though the total population of metropolitan areas has been increasing fairly slowly, the urbanized land area has grown rapidly. This low-density development brings many problems, including suburban congestion, loss of open space, and increased infrastructure costs.

One of the themes that have emerged in this book is the persistent tilt of economic policy toward rural areas and suburbs. The widening gap between rich and poor has favored affluent suburban residents over those who live in the cities, and Michigan's tax policies have exacerbated the trend. Also, local school districts must rely exclusively on local property taxes for their capital expenditures. Thus, the poorest urban districts are unable to provide adequate facilities for their schoolchildren, even though the districts often have high property-tax rates. This accelerates the flight to the suburbs. Also, the funding formula for highways is strongly slanted in favor of lightly populated rural counties. And the "Headlee Amendment" restricts the ability of local jurisdictions to raise property-tax revenue, but it favors regions with new growth over older areas that are already urbanized. When taken together, all of these policies contribute to a situation in which rural and suburban areas in Michigan are favored, and cities (especially older, poorer cities) are penalized. *Michigan should treat older, developed areas on a more equal basis with undeveloped and newly developing areas.*

Environmental Policies

Until the 1960s and early 1970s, neither Michigan nor the rest of the United States had much in the way of an environmental policy. Since then, however, an increased environmental awareness has led to state and federal policy initiatives in many areas. Many sources of air pollution have been reduced, as has phosphorus pollution in the Great Lakes. Michigan is one of the nation's leaders with its deposit-and-return system for bottles and cans. The trend toward destruction of wetlands has been slowed down. Nevertheless, a number of challenges remain for environmental policy.

Some environmental problems are beyond the reach of policies that could be enacted in Michigan. For example, global warming from greenhouse gas emissions will only be solved through policies that are coordinated internationally. But some problems will continue to be addressed at the state and local levels, as well as at the federal and international levels. One of these problems is contamination of groundwater and sediments. The key to success in this area does not come so much in the form of a particular policy. Instead, the key is to recognize that complete elimination of contaminants is prohibitively expensive. Rather than engaging in a doomed effort to eliminate contamination completely, the best policy is to identify the sites that pose the greatest risk to the public health, and to find cost-effective methods of dealing with those sites.

Corrections Policies

In the 1980s and 1990s, prisons were the fastest-growing sector of the Michigan economy. It is possible that the people of Michigan are safer with more prisoners behind bars. Nevertheless, our incarceration policies are very expensive, and this leads to a recommendation: *Consider making greater use of probation, halfway houses, and electronic monitoring as alternatives to incarceration.*

Partly as a result of long prison sentences, the incarceration rate is substantially higher in Michigan than in neighboring states. If the incarceration rate were the same in Michigan as in other states in the region, Michigan's prison spending would be reduced by about $500 million per year. It is not clear that the high rate of imprisonment is worth it. I am not suggesting that we consider changes in the policies toward the most violent criminal offenders. However, for some offenders, alternative methods of punishment have the potential to provide security for the public at considerably lower cost.

Health-Care and Health-Insurance Policies

We discussed health care and health insurance in chapter 4. For health-care policy and health-insurance policy, perhaps the most important thing is for the public to understand the situation. New medical technologies have led to large reductions in death rates, but these advances have not come cheaply. The trend toward higher health-care expenses is expected to continue for many years to come. This is partly because the population is aging, and partly because medical research is expected to continue to produce new medicines, new techniques, and new devices. These new developments will save lives, but many of them will be expensive. If we are to take advantage of the new developments, *someone* will *somehow* have to pay for them. Hard choices will have to be made.

It is likely that some of the difficult choices will be made (for better or worse) at the federal level. But some choices will be made by individuals and policymakers in Michigan. Individuals make choices every day about diet, exercise, and other factors that have an impact on health and health care. For policymakers in Michigan, one of the biggest issues will be how to handle the burgeoning Medicaid program (assuming that the current division of Medicaid responsibility between the states and the federal government is maintained). It will be necessary either to raise taxes, or to cut other areas of spending, or to reduce the number of people eligible for Medicaid, or to reduce expenditures per Medicaid recipient.

One recent policy development should be watched carefully. Massachusetts recently instituted a plan that combines incentives for employers to provide health insurance, incentives for individuals to acquire health insurance, penalties for those who do not get insurance, and expanded eligibility for Medicaid. In a few years, this program is projected to achieve nearly universal health-insurance coverage for the people of Massachusetts. If the Massachusetts program proves successful, other states (including Michigan) may consider following suit. Of course, if the Massachusetts program proves successful, it would probably be better for the federal government to institute similar reforms nationally.

Labor-Market Policies

Over the long term, the best way to ensure a healthy labor market in Michigan is to provide our residents with education so they will have the skills to succeed in the global economy of today and tomorrow. Education was discussed in chapter 2. However, we also discussed several other labor-market policies in chapter 4. That discussion led to some recommendations:

- *Institute a state supplement to the federal Earned Income Tax Credit (EITC).* Studies have shown that the EITC leads to an increase in employment. This stands in contrast to the minimum wage, which increases the earnings of some workers while making it harder for others to find work. Another advantage of the EITC is that it is targeted toward people in low-income families, whereas many of those who benefit from an increased minimum wage are in affluent families.

- *Continue to refine the system of Unemployment Insurance taxation.* In Michigan, the base for the employer payroll tax for Unemployment Insurance (UI) is the first $9,000 of each employee's earnings for the year. This tax base is a much higher fraction of the earnings of low-wage workers than of high-wage workers. If the tax base were increased, the tax rate could be reduced. The UI taxes are "experience rated," which means that tax rates are higher for employers with a history of lots of layoffs. However, the system of experience rating is imperfect, so that high-layoff employers are still subsidized by low-layoff employers. The experience-rating system could be made more complete. Finally, in 2005, Michigan took steps to rein in the practice of "dumping," by which some employers have been able to evade UI taxes in the past. As we gain experience with the new rules, we should evaluate their performance to make sure they have succeeded in reducing dumping.

Welfare Policies

The best antipoverty policies have nothing to do with public-assistance programs. In the long run, by far the most important antipoverty policies have to do with education. The Earned Income Tax Credit, mentioned above, is another policy that can have a large positive effect on low-income families. In any event, however, Michigan does have a substantial low-income population. In 2004, about 1.3 million Michigan residents were in poverty, according to the official poverty definition used by the federal government. Alleviation of poverty is one of the major goals of public-assistance policies and other policies for low-income families, which were discussed in chapter 4.

The policy landscape changed dramatically in the early and middle 1990s, when Michigan and several other states enacted welfare reforms. The biggest change of all came with the federal government's reforms in 1996. These reforms emphasized work requirements for those receiving benefits. These changes led to a very large decrease in the number of families receiving welfare payments, both in Michigan and nationwide. So far, these more restrictive policies have not led to a substantial upsurge in poverty. The fear remains, however, that the current system will not perform well if the economy should experience a severe recession.

The following are among the policies that have the potential to help those residents who are in or near poverty status:

- *Improved public transportation;*
- *Streamlined procedures for assessment and referral* for welfare recipients who have mental-health or substance-abuse problems;
- *Community service jobs;* and
- *Greater use of supported-work situations* in which enhanced supervision is provided for those who have difficulty in making the transition to work.

Tax Policies

We have discussed taxation in several chapters in this book. However, most of the discussion of taxes was concentrated in chapter 5. Several recommendations came out of that discussion:

- *Make the income tax more progressive.* I have emphasized the fact that the tax system in Michigan has exacerbated the trend toward greater inequality by putting relatively more of the tax burden on the shoulders of middle-income and low-income people. The income tax can help to reverse this trend, because the income tax is the only tax that is levied on the basis of ability to pay. Michigan's income tax is unusual in that it has only a single flat tax rate on all taxable income. A second rate in the income tax is the best way to shift some of the tax burden away from those at the bottom of the income scale (although instituting a second rate would require a constitutional amendment). Another way to make the income tax more progressive, without instituting a second rate, would be to increase both the personal exemption and the single tax rate. If the Michigan income tax were changed in one of these ways, a substantial part of the additional tax revenue would actually be paid by residents of other states, because state and local income taxes are deductible from the federal income tax.

- *Extend the sales tax to a greater variety of services.* Michigan exempts most services from taxation. (In fact, Michigan exempts even more services than are exempted by most states.) Services have grown rapidly in recent decades, so that services account for an ever-growing portion of the economy. Thus, the revenue losses from nontaxation of services have increased over the years. If the sales tax in Michigan is broadened to include more services, it will be possible to raise additional revenues while reducing the sales-tax rate from its current rate of 6 percent. This will also reduce the current inequitable difference between the taxation of goods and the taxation of services.
- *Remove the assessment cap in the property tax.* Since 1994, Michigan has limited the amount by which the taxable value of a property can increase from year to year. (However, properties are reassessed to their full value when they are sold.) The "assessment cap" erodes the revenue-raising capability of the property tax. It also creates an inequity, because a property that has been sold recently will pay much higher taxes than a comparable property that has been held by the same owner for many years. Removal of the assessment cap would fix these problems. If there is a desire to keep the overall amount of property-tax revenue from increasing too rapidly, removal of the cap could be coupled with a reduction in property-tax rates.
- *Convert the excise taxes on beer, wine, tobacco products, and motor fuels to a percentage of the sales price.* Most tax revenues come from taxes that are levied as a percentage of a dollar value. However, the selective excise taxes are "unit taxes." For example, the cigarette tax is levied as a number of dollars per pack. Over time, inflation will erode the real revenue-raising capability of a unit tax, unless the tax rate is raised explicitly. The tax rate on cigarettes has been raised substantially, so the only need for the cigarette tax is to convert to a percentage basis. The taxes on beer and wine have stayed at the same nominal level for decades. Thus, for beer and wine, the tax rates should be increased, and the taxes should also be converted to a percentage basis. The tax rates on diesel fuel and gasoline should be equalized and increased, and both should be converted to a percentage basis.
- *Repeal the Single Business Tax (SBT), but only if the revenues are replaced fully, and not with a corporate tax.* In its original form, the SBT had many attractive features. Over the years, however, the SBT has been damaged by a large number of exemptions, deductions, and other distortions. Even now, a case

can be made for keeping the SBT and trying to strengthen it. In my judgment, however, it would be better to repeal the SBT, but only if the revenues are replaced. To repeal the SBT without replacing the revenues would be fiscally irresponsible to an extraordinary degree.

Moreover, if the SBT is replaced, care should be taken in choosing the replacement tax. It has been suggested that the SBT should be replaced with a corporate tax, but this would be a mistake. A corporate tax causes more economic distortions than a tax like the SBT, and it generates a stream of revenues that is more volatile over time. The best candidates for replacing the SBT revenues are extensions of the income tax and/or the sales tax.

Policies to Strengthen Michigan's Democracy

Because of the long decline of manufacturing, Michigan's economy would be facing very serious challenges at this time regardless of our economic policies. In addition, economic policies in Michigan are often short-sighted and counterproductive. The main purpose of this book has been to suggest some ways to improve those policies. However, regardless of how much solid analysis is offered by me and by other economists, Michigan's economic policies can only be changed through the political process. If the political system does not respond, then the economy of Michigan will continue to slide down the unfortunate track of the last 30 years.

In my view, the political system in Michigan is not completely broken. That's the good news. However, the bad news is that our political system certainly does not function very well. Before closing, I would like to offer some thoughts about how to improve the political system.

• *Relax term limits.* I became a member of the faculty at Michigan State University in 1983. By the time I had been on the job for six years, I had published a book and some articles, and I had improved my teaching techniques. I was off to a decent start, but I was still not nearly as effective as I would be after gaining more years of experience. In any complex job, it takes time to learn how to do things better. (That is why workers with a lot of experience typically earn so much more than inexperienced workers. In fact, the typical wage premium for experienced workers has increased sharply in the last few decades.) And yet, because of term limits, members of the Michigan House of Representatives are forced to move on after only six years on the job. This means that many of the people making vital decisions about Michigan are re-markably inexperienced. Nowhere else in our society is so much responsibil-ity given routinely to people with so little experience.

I must make clear that I *do* believe in term limits for members of the Michi-gan legislature (and for members of Congress as well). If there were no term limits, a legislator in a safe district could serve for decades on end. It would be easy for such a legislator to become stale and corrupt, and/or to lose touch with his or her constituents. But even though term limits are a good thing, it is possible to have too much of a good thing. Right now, Michigan has far too much of the good thing called term limits.

I believe that the current legislative term limits in Michigan should be re-laxed. My preference for the maximum length of service in the legislature is 24 years. However, I am not deeply invested in any particular number. In today's legislature, *any* increase in term limits, no matter how small, would be a step in the right direction.

• *End gerrymandering of legislative districts.* Term limits are an important issue. However, term limits are probably not as important as the way in which legislative district boundaries are drawn. The practice of drawing district boundaries to benefit a particular group is called "gerrymandering."[1] In recent years, computers have made it possible for politicians to engage in gerryman-dering with unprecedented precision.

In a gerrymandering scheme, the party that controls the legislature will strategically redraw the district boundaries so as to herd the voters into un-competitive districts. Gerrymandering has two poisonous side effects. First, a gerrymandered legislature may be fairly unrepresentative. In the extreme case, the party that controls the legislature at the time of redistricting may be able to maintain its grip on power, even if it does not have the support of a majority of voters.

The second side effect is even worse. Gerrymandering works by concen-trating voters into relatively uncompetitive districts, even when it would be possible to have competitive districts. In the Michigan legislature, as in the U.S. House of Representatives, gerrymandering means that most voters are either in safe Republican districts or safe Democratic districts. In safe, un-competitive districts, politicians from the dominant party have little reason to appeal to moderate voters, because they can rely on the overwhelming power of their own party faithful. In fact, any attempt to appeal to moderate voters may be harmful to the career of a politician in an uncompetitive district, because it might incur the wrath of the extreme elements of his or her party. Thus, uncompetitive districts are more likely to elect representatives from the extremes of the political spectrum. Consequently, the governing body has relatively few voices from the middle, even though most voters actually reside fairly close to the center of the political spectrum. Moderate voters are underrepresented, while the more extreme elements are overrepresented.

One solution to the gerrymandering problem is to remove politicians from the redistricting process. Some proposals involve placing redistricting in the hands of a nonpartisan panel of retired judges, with explicit instructions to avoid gerrymandering. If Michigan were to adopt this kind of system, we would have many more meaningful, competitive races than we have now. The legislature would be more truly representative of the people of Michigan.

Putting a nonpartisan panel in charge of the redistricting process is an idea that the people of Michigan should consider seriously. However, it is not the only way to deal with gerrymandering. A second possible reform involves a system of proportional representation.

We are accustomed to the idea of a legislature in which every member has exactly one vote. However, it is perfectly possible to have a different system, under which different members of the legislature would have different numbers of votes. In each district, the two candidates with the most votes in the general election would both win a seat in the legislature. For example, consider a district where the Republican candidate receives 53 percent of the vote, and the Democratic candidate receives 47 percent. Each of the candidates would go to the legislature. The Republican would be able to cast 0.53 votes in the legislature, and the Democrat would be able to cast 0.47 votes.

Under our current system, elections to the legislature are "winner-take-all." When the winner takes all, the drawing of district boundaries can make a huge difference. Under the proposed system of proportional representation, however, the district boundaries would not be nearly as important.

Will Michigan's Economy Have a Brighter Future?

There is plenty of reason for concern about the Michigan economy, which has not performed as well as the economy of the United States as a whole. Unless Michigan makes some policy changes, we can expect more of the same. However, there is also plenty of reason for hope. One reason for hope is that economic policy is getting a lot of attention in Michigan. If you are reading these words, you are interested in the Michigan economy. Even though the public still has a very incomplete understanding of the situation, I sense an increase in public awareness that the dogmas of the past are not working. Much of the discussion of public policies in Michigan is still characterized by a lethargic complacency, but it seems to me that more of Michigan's people are beginning to look to the future in a serious way.

Of course, even if the people of Michigan develop a stronger understanding of their economic situation, it does not necessarily mean that we will see better public policies. Our current policies are the result of a political process. In cases where entrenched interests have benefited from the policies of the past, they will lobby hard to protect their privileges. The fight for improved economic policies in Michigan will not be easy, but I am cautiously optimistic that improvements will be made.

Some of the policy proposals in this book are probably familiar to many people who have followed the policy debate in Michigan. But I imagine that some of the proposals are new to many, and I recognize that it usually takes time for new ideas to gain wide acceptance. But I remain hopeful that even some of the newest ideas described here will flourish. After all, it was once considered radical to say that women or blacks should be allowed to vote, but the idea of universal suffrage is no longer radical at all.

I began this chapter with words written by Abraham Lincoln during the Civil War. I end it with words written by the great British economist John Maynard Keynes, during the Great Depression. Keynes laid much of the foundation for modern macroeconomics in his 1935 book *The General Theory of Employment, Interest, and Money*. Toward the end of the book, Keynes wrote of his hope that his ideas would eventually have an influence on economic policy. My contribution here is small compared with that of Keynes, but I cannot refrain from recalling Keynes's words:

If the ideas are correct . . . it would be a mistake, I predict, to dispute their po-
tency over a period of time . . . The ideas of economists and philosophers,
both when they are right and when they are wrong, are more powerful than
is commonly understood . . . I am sure that the power of vested interests is
vastly exaggerated compared with the gradual encroachment of ideas.[2]

NOTES

1. Elbridge Gerry was governor of Massachusetts in 1812, at the time of a redistricting
   scheme that favored the Republican Party over the Federalist Party. A cartoonist drew one
   of the oddly shaped legislative districts to look like a salamander. The phrase "Gerrymandering" was born from "Gerry" and "salamander."
2. John Maynard Keynes, *The General Theory of Employment, Interest, and Money* (New York: Har-
   court, Brace & World, 1964), 383–84.

Index

R

rail systems, 85, 86

Rainy Day Fund, 105

Reagan, Ronald, 115

recessions, budgetary problems caused by, 102

recycling programs, 92, 93, 97

retirement plans, 78–79n.32

road commissions, county, 83, 96, 177

roads, Michigan: federal funding of, 82, 84; gross weight limit on, 83, 84, 96, 177; ownership of, 82–83, 96, 176–77; policy recommendations for improving, 83–84, 96–97, 176–77; poor quality of, xx, 81, 82, 83, 96, 176; rural bias of funding for, 82, 83, 84–85, 91, 96, 97, 176, 178; state funding of, 82, 83, 84–85, 91, 96, 97; unpaved, 98n.1

Ryan, Earl, 101

S

sales tax: on business-to-business sales, 135, 161n.14; erosion of base of, 134–37, 157; federal deductibility of, 146, 158, 164n.28, 164n.30; on food, 136–37; increases in, 129, 146, 158; as percentage tax, 98n.3, 139; as proportion of total tax revenues, 128, 129; and Proposal A, 60, 129; as regressive tax, 142, 144; and services, xxi, 122, 134–36, 154, 157, 158, 182; states without, 160n.2

Sands, Gary, 87, 89, 91

School Aid Fund, 107, 132

school year, length of, 68–69, 79n.38, 174

Seefeldt, Kristin, 116, 117

service sector, importance of in Michigan's

economy, 2, 3, 9–10, 135

Silicon Valley, 54

Single Business Tax (SBT): abatements to, 164n.33; and business location decisions, 148, 151; and capital investments, 150–51, 160; exemption for small businesses, 143, 151; phase-out of, 12, 152–54, 160, 175, 183–84; policy options for, 152–54; reductions in rate of, 134, 157; stability of, 150; tax base of, 130

Slemrod, Joel, 134, 146

Smoot-Hawley Tariff Act, the, 26

solid waste, 93–94, 97–98

Southeast Michigan Council of Governments (SEMCOG), 23, 31n.16

State Education Tax, 129

state equalized value, 154

Streamlined Sales Tax Project (SSTP), 136

suburbs, 88–89, 90, 97, 177

Superfund Law, 92

T

tax expenditures, 135

Tax Reform Act of 1986, 146

taxes: Alternative Minimum, 163–64n.27; and business location decisions, 11–12, 148–49, 175; centralization of, in Michigan, 128–29, 157, 160n.5; decline in revenues of, xviii, 132, 133, 157, 172; effect of inflation on, 139, 140; effects on different income classes, 141–44, 161n.7, 163n.25; eroding base of, xvii–xviii, 132, 172; exemptions in, 137, 141, 159, 161n.7, 162n.16, 163n.25; exporting of, 145–48, 158, 163–64n.27; "Fair," 154; federal deductibility of, 142, 145–46, 148, 158, 163–64n.27,

MICHIGAN'S
ECONOMIC
FUTURE